ESTABLISHING

Your *Course*

Through The

PROPHETIC ANOINTING

An easy to follow guide for the believer and local church in the function and demonstration of the prophetic.

PASTOR BARRY A. COOK

Establishing Your Course Through the Prophetic Anointing
ISBN:1-890820-03-2

If you would like further information regarding the author, please write to:

Barry A. Cook
Embassy Family Church
4055 Oceanside Boulevard, Suite T
Oceanside, CA 92056

Published & Copyright ©1998
Battlecry Press
4055 Oceanside Boulevard, Suite T
Oceanside, CA 92056

Endorsements

"Barry has a message the entire body of Christ desperately needs. God has poured valuable revelation into this uncommon man of God whose work is a model of what God wants in this generation."

Dr. Mike Murdock
Mike Murdock Ministries, Dallas, TX

"Barry Cook is a powerful preacher with a spirit of revival and reformation burning in his heart. He is a man of intensity and integrity and I believe (this book) will be a blessing to any (believer or) ministry..."

Pastor Michael Pitts
Cornerstone Church, Toledo, OH

"The territorial, apostolic mantle and mindset that rests on Barry Cook is what is desperately needed in this generation to develop leaders, not to pastor congregations, but to pastor territories."

J. Konrad Hölé
World Dominion Ministries, Minneapolis, MN

"In every generation God raises up generals to lead His army. Pastor Barry A. Cook is such a man. His spiritual insight far exceeds his years, and his revelatory and prophetic teaching will impact many lives for years to come."

Bishop Brian Keith Williams
All Nations Church, Columbus, OH

ACKNOWLEDGEMENTS

A special thanks goes to all the faithful saints in the Body of Christ who have been such a valuable part of helping to make this book a reality. Many thanks go especially to Belinda Dover, Tammy Strakos, Jayme Hix, and Hosanna Haughton. Thank you for the endless hours of dedication you put into this project. There are great rewards ahead for you all. God will richly bless you and return a great harvest to you for the seeds you have sown.

To my wife, Terri, I love you! You are my friend and my partner. You believed in me when no one else did. Thanks for all those little extra touches that you added to this book and my life. Most of all, thanks for believing in and supporting the plan of God for OUR lives together. The best is yet to come!

CONTENTS

"...for the testimony of Jesus is the spirit of prophecy."
(Revelation 19:10b)

"To be desired above all gifts is prophecy. Why prophecy? Because prophecy by the power of the Spirit is the only power that saves humanity. Prophecy is to be coveted above all things, and every person has to have it. Now every person may have (different) gifts, but everybody has prophecy."

Smith Wigglesworth

"Pursue love, and desire spiritual gifts, but especially that you may prophesy." (I Corinthians 14:1)

Forward

It is my prayer that through this book you may be stirred to a new hunger for spiritual gifts and all the blessings that accompany the demonstration of the power of the Holy Ghost.

I want to begin by clarifying that the prophetic is not the only spiritual dimension that needs to be added to the church, but it is the particular topic that this book will focus on. This book is not meant to be a comprehensive study of the anointing and operation of the prophetic, but rather a tool used for the activation of the prophetic in the church and the personal lives of those in the Body of Christ.

For years, I have had a deep, immense desire to gain supernatural insight into the present day function of the apostolic and prophetic. In the early days of my ministry the prophetic mantle would come upon me and my eyes would be opened, and the knowings of God would come to me. Unfortunately, it seemed like my attempts to operate in the prophetic brought me more troubles than it did blessings to the people of God.

Throughout my years of ministry, God has shown me various reasons for these results. In this book, I have endeavored to bring revelation to the root causes of these reactions. We will discuss such contributing factors as:

1) **Undeveloped character;**
2) **Incorrect thinking that the gift supersedes common courtesy and respect for others;**
3) **Missing God's timing;**
4) **Lacking wisdom and a spirit of grace to season the word;**
5) **Assuming that the gift caused others to overlook the error in my own life.**

When the prophetic, or a spirit of prophecy, would come upon me (through touching someone's hand, looking at a person or a picture, while praying for someone, etc.), details of their life would unfold before my eyes. The details of what I saw would be so accurate that they were undeniable. The problems came because the word would be so exact that no one would ever rebuke me or correct me for the mixtures that I carried inside of me. As a result of **character flaws, soulish mixtures,** and a **lack of prophetic fathering,** combined with **rejection** and **insecurity** that had been received over time, I began to try to **press down and even ignore the prophetic promptings of the Spirit in order to avoid "trouble."** I tried to just be a normal, nice preacher. I began to realize that I must first work on the improvement of my character, and by doing so I would become more mature and seasoned in the prophetic flow.

After many years of my own frustrated efforts to push down what came so natural to me, I had become bound by a **fear of failure**. This fear of failure was present even though everything else in my life seemed to be properly in order according to God's will for me and my family. However, I still longed to fill the void inside and find accuracy to flow and operate in the prophetic anointing, because I knew it was a part of me. I was fighting confusion and dissatisfaction as fast as I could through prayer and Word study. **It was during that time period that something happened to me that would change my life forever.**

On January 23, 1995 at 2:30 in the afternoon, I had a visitation from the Lord. I was in prayer in my room and I was suddenly interrupted. I looked up to see Jesus standing in my room. It was a glorious time! **He began to speak to me about the prophetic and its true purposes of building, establishing, confirming and setting a course as a spiritual operation of the Kingdom of God.** The Lord spent most of the time, however, speaking to me about the apostolic anointing, its common misconceptions and present-day mindsets that were wrong in its application. He completed His visit with me by speaking to me about the grace of God and the five-fold operation in detail.

This visitation lasted probably about two hours, but it seemed like time stood still.

As a result of my time with the Lord and our discussion of the apostolic, I prepared to write about the apostolic anointing, but the Spirit of the Lord came upon me and instructed me *to "first lay the foundation of the prophetic anointing."* Today it is popular to call ourselves prophetic people or to refer to our churches as an apostolic church, but the truth of the matter is that we have never really functioned in the prophetic to the degree needed to move on to the apostolic. The time has come when the church must begin prophesying and speaking forth what God wants, and not what man wants. We need to stop being a part of religious arguments and start speaking the life changing Word of the Lord. Our words should contain such power that they shake the nation, right up to the governmental offices.

God <u>first</u> desires for the prophetic ministry to encourage believers to repent and become seriously committed to the Lord. He **<u>then</u>** will use the prophetic word to build us up and make us stronger and bolder so that we can take our proper position in the Body of Christ. **<u>After</u>** accuracy and integrity has been established, we are able to prophesy beyond the walls of the church **so that the Word of God effects people in society around us, from the highest to the lowest. As a result, God will then be able to change our cities and our nation.**

If you read about the people God has used throughout church history, you will notice that they were not the kind of people who sat at home twiddling their thumbs, apologizing for their opinions. <u>**Instead**</u>**, they were men and women who rose up in the power of the Holy Spirit and acted as battering rams for the Lord.**

The greater the level of backsliding, the more powerful the prophetic ministry must be. The more stiff-necked the people are, the stronger the prophetic anointing that is required. **But, the prophetic anointing cannot be tainted with sinful and soulish mixtures or the results will be to only oppose the true purpose and plan of God.**

We should not preach just to get a general hallelujah reaction, but instead to see results and the progression of God's Kingdom. **We should desire to influence people, not in a natural, human manner, but by the Holy Spirit.** We must refuse to watch our nation perish. We must refuse to accept a backslidden Body of Christ. We must refuse to accept a watered down gospel. Neither can we accept a presentation of the gospel that is cute or completely palatable. The gospel must be presented as it really is. We should not be willing to accept anything but the glory and the power of God in demonstration. **The message is the same today as it was in the days of Jeremiah:** *"Land, Land, here the word of the Lord!"*

"When a prophet prophesies it will do more than edify, exhort and comfort. It can also impart spiritual grace into individuals and assemblies."

John Eckhardt

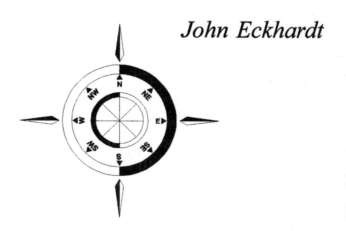

PART I

The Supply of the Spirit

Chapter 1

Supply and Demand

"For I know that this will turn out for my deliverance through your prayer and the <u>supply of the Spirit</u> of Jesus Christ,

according to my earnest expectation and hope that in nothing I shall be ashamed, but that with all boldness, as always, so now also Christ will be magnified in my body, whether by life or by death.

For to me, to live is Christ, and to die is gain." (Philippians 1:19-21)

Every believer has a supply of the Spirit. We see this in Philippians 1:19. The apostle Paul says, *"I know this will turn out for my deliverance, through your prayer and the <u>supply of the Spirit</u> of Jesus Christ..."*

Drawing from the supply of the anointing from ministry gifts, and drawing from the supply of the anointing from one another as believers is a principle that we as a church and a people, have to understand. We have to begin drawing and learning how to draw from the anointing of God. Each one of us has a different type of gifting. Not only the gifts and calling in us as individuals, but also the gifts of the five-fold ministry as seen in Ephesians chapter 4. Each one has a different supply of the Spirit.

We are all reservoirs for the supply of the Spirit. That's why each one of us has something that someone else needs. We all have something that we can give to one another. When we are born again, and Spirit-filled, we receive a supply of the Spirit of God. <u>All believers</u>, as well as those who in are ministry positions, have a supply of the Spirit. You have to make a demand on the anointing on someone else's life. You've got to make a "pull" or a "withdrawal" on the ministry gift.

The Body of Christ can no longer just respond as spectators when we come to church. We've got to pull and draw, desiring to pull virtue out of the ministry gift that's being poured out.

For instance, when someone gives out a word from the Lord or operates in prophecy, we should not just sit back and say to ourselves, "Oh that's nice." When we do that we miss out on a blessing for our life because there is a supply of the Spirit that could be supplied to build your own faith, your own joy and your own strength, and to help you become more established and planted. That is why you have to draw from the Spirit. It's our responsibility to draw.

PUTTING A DEMAND ON THE ANOINTING

> *"And suddenly, a woman who had a flow of blood for twelve years came from behind and touched the hem of His garment.*
> *For she said to herself, "If I may only touch His garment, I shall be made well." (Matt. 9:20,21)*

The Bible goes on to say that Jesus turned around and said, *"I perceive that virtue (or power) came out of Me."* He didn't even see the lady coming, but she reached out and she made a demand on His anointing. It's your responsibility to draw on the anointing. You can pull on the anointing by your faith. **Your faith is not in the person, but your faith is in the Spirit of God within that person.** You can pull an anointing out of people by your hunger and your faith that will strengthen you, increase you, and will add to you the things that you are lacking.

That is the difference between people who sit in church for years and remain dead, (with no zeal or progressive relationship with God) and people who are able to change, grow, mature, and begin to come into the blessings of God quickly. There will always be a supply when there is a demand.

> *"And behold, two blind men sitting by the road, when they heard that Jesus was passing by, cried out saying, "Have mercy on us O Lord, Son of David!"*
>
> *Then the multitude warned them that they should be quite. But they cried out all the more saying, "Have mercy on us, O Lord, Son of David!" (Matthew 20:30,31)*

If those blind men had not put a demand on Him, He would have passed them by. Jesus was just walking by, they heard He was coming, and they cried out, "Lord, have mercy, have mercy!" The multitudes responded saying, "Be quiet."

Sometimes you might be in a place where the people or the atmosphere says, "Be quiet." The atmosphere might be saying, "Sleep." The environment might be saying, "Just try and do your best to get to church and if you get there that's enough, at least you got there."

It's not enough to just be a warm body filling up a room. That will not supply you with what you need in your life from the Spirit of God. You have to make a demand from the Spirit. You need to be hungry and seek after God. The Bible says that, ***"They cried out all the more."*** That means **the more they had resistance, the more they said, "No, I'll focus, I'll receive, I'll pull, I'll grab, I'll get everything that I need."** And we've got to have that same attitude as well. If a prophecy goes out that may be directly for someone else, but you feel it applies to your life, then you better grab it and claim that promise for your own life. The Bible says that *the Spirit of prophecy is the testimony of Christ.* In Christ your need will be met. When the Word of the Lord goes forth it is freely given for the profit of all.

> ***"The Spirit of the Lord is upon Me,***
> ***Because He has anointed Me***
> ***To preach the gospel to the poor;***
> ***He has sent Me to heal the brokenhearted,***
> ***To proclaim liberty to the captives***
> ***And recovery of sight to the blind,***
> ***To set at liberty those who are oppressed,***

To proclaim the acceptable year of the Lord." (Luke 4:18,19)

We put a demand on the anointing by our faith. Faith ignites spiritual gifts. Faith ignites healing, it ignites personal words of wisdom and knowledge or prophecy. There are some of you who come to the house of God with a need for someone to come to you and say something like this, "I'm just feeling like God is saying to you that on Tuesday, when you go to that particular job interview, that it's going to be the right place for you." That person didn't even know anything about your schedule for Tuesday. All of a sudden, that prophetic word comes forth and ignites your faith, it builds you up. That's how the Body of Christ is supposed to be.

STIR UP THE GIFT

Another way to make a demand on the anointing is stated in II Timothy 1:6, *"...stir up the gift of God which is in you..."*

The church should be full of people who are stirred up for God. Every usher, every altar worker, every classroom, every house call that's made, should be a result of people who are stirring up the gift of God within themselves. When that occurs, then there is a release of the anointing. They're releasing a prophetic utterance, they're releasing a move of the Spirit, and they're releasing the gifts of the Spirit.

That's the way we should be living our own lives. It's your responsibility to stir up your own gift. As a minister, I can't just say, "Well, we had another service and nobody pulled on me." I've heard preachers say that before. That's called lazy and having no faith at all. **However, some congregations are too passive, not expecting anything. We need to resist passivity on all sides.**

In Luke 4, it says that there were *many lepers in the land and none were healed.* Jesus is relating to their level of faith during the time of Elijah. There was no one that put a demand on the anointing. We must value the anointing and giftings in one another. **Where there is no demand, there is no supply.**

If you make a demand on the Spirit of God, He will speak to you. If you make a demand on the Spirit of God, He will give you confirmation in the spirit. If you are pulling on, and making a demand on the Spirit of God, He will give you a word, and He will give you revelation out of the scripture. The key is to make a demand on Him.

THE DANGER OF UNBELIEF

"But Jesus said to them, 'A prophet is not without honor except in his own

*country, among his own relatives, and
in his own house.'
    Now He could do no mighty work
there, except that He laid His hands upon
a few sick people and healed them."
(Mark 6:4-5)*

In Luke chapter 4, the Bible reveals that because
of unbelief there was a lack of the supply of the Spirit.
Jesus stood up and He said, *"I am anointed to preach
the gospel, I've come to heal the blind, to set at liberty
those who are oppressed, those who are down trodden."*
Unfortunately, it says later in that chapter that He could
only heal a few people at that place because the people
said among themselves, "Isn't this just the carpenter's
boy? Who is this guy? He's just a carpenter. He's
nothing."

Maybe you have experienced that same lack of
faith in your church or city. **However, as a group of
believers, you can increase the anointing to bring a
change by continuing to make a demand on the
Spirit of God every time you come together.** Luke
4:18-19 is within all of us. Every one of us has that
same reservoir inside.

So that means, if I'm pulling on your reservoir
and you're pulling on my reservoir, we're all pulling on
one another's reservoir, then we're going to have an
explosion of the anointing of God in our midst.

Remember, you have got to make a demand. It's your responsibility to make that demand.

In the midst of these people was a supply, a reservoir of salvation, healing, deliverance and miracles. The problem was that they didn't see Jesus as a reservoir. They just saw Him as another man, just somebody else, just a carpenter. We can't ever have an entertainment or a spectator mentality in church. Every time you come to church, you must place a demand on the anointing.

The woman with the issue of blood pressed through the multitude to touch Jesus and He didn't even see her coming. You don't have to make a big announcement about your needs or what you're going to do or not do. You just need to come with your spirit set in motion to receive, and you will.

> *"And Jesus, immediately knowing in Himself that power had gone out of Him, turned around in the crowd and said, 'Who touched My clothes?'*
> *But His disciples said to Him, 'You see the multitude thronging you, and you say, 'Who touched Me?"(Mark 5:30-31)*

Faith releases the anointing, unbelief blocks it. You've got to reach out with your faith. You can't have a passive attitude. You can draw from the anointing of God in your prayer time. That's the difference between having an anointed prayer time and a dry, boring prayer time. It depends upon the way that you are pursuing that draw. You can draw by faith from the well of the Spirit of prayer.

> *"But Jesus said, 'Somebody touched Me, for I perceived power (or virtue) going out from Me.'"* *(Luke 8:46)*

The definition of **"virtue"** is: power, strength, ability and might.

> *"When she heard about Jesus, she came behind Him in the crowd and touched His garment."* *(Mark 5:27)*

She "heard" about Him. That's what I want to point out from this scripture. All she did was hear. **Passive people do not receive. Hungry souls receive, and draw out virtue or power.** All can be used by God and all can receive from God if you are hungry enough to pursue Him.

IT'S UP TO YOU

In Acts 28:8-10, we see that the apostle Paul performed many signs and wonders in that region and he said that the people there, *"honored us in many ways."*

Let me illustrate this point. When ministering overseas, it's common to see people who have walked for days and even miles to get to a service. Because of their pursuit, they receive something from the Lord while they are there. This is because for days beforehand, they began to set themselves in motion. They know that if they can just get to that meeting and make a demand on the ministry gift that's going to be there, they will receive what they need from God.

However, many American believers won't even walk two blocks. People in other countries seem to understand that everything their salvation, their deliverance, and even their prosperity, depends on the demand of their faith. Their little girl, their husband, their wife, their marriage, everything depends on God. They know they need to pull, because they believe that something is going to be given to them by the Spirit of God.

In Acts 5:15 it says, **"...they brought forth the sick."** The phrase "brought forth" is critical there. The people had to go out of their way to bring people to the apostles. It says that they brought beds out in the street and people out on stretchers. Not only were the people that were bringing the sick and lame moving in faith, but those that needed a healing were moving in faith as well, so they <u>all</u> pulled on the gift of God.

You see, **there are things available to you from heaven right now, today, this very moment, that are yours to meet the needs in your life.** If you make a

will supply to you. Wherever
gathered together in His name,
idst of them, ready to minister
r faith pulls the supply out into

lls about men tearing off the roof
:mber, they tore the roof off and
oom. They were making a demand
he Bible says that the place was
in the middle of His sermon, and
off the house. They were hungry!
; a demand on the Spirit of God.
hurch gets back to the book of Acts,
tate that the church was intended to be
e ready to be the Bride of Christ. Many
1 this, but it's a whole different thing to
making such bold proclamations as,
ord is fulfilled in your ears." We must
e word of God is true and applicable today.
the benefits He paid a price for are available
ight now.

herever there is a demand
there will be a supply!

Chapter 2

Understanding the Prophetic

There are three main times that God sends a prophetic or apostolic anointing into churches:

1.   At the beginning.
2.   At the point of a transition.
3.   At the end.

The church is founded on the apostolic and prophetic anointing. A church that is not founded on those things is not following Biblical pattern.

For instance, a pastoral gift may be able to go into a particular territory that has a spiritually open atmosphere and it would be easy for him or her to gather a crowd of people or build a church.

When the heavens are open, you can walk in, begin preaching, and the manifestation of God begin to happen. Under an open heaven, the gifts of the spirit are free to flow, and that includes prophecy.

I Corinthians 14:1 says, *"Pursue love, and desire spiritual gifts, but especially that you may prophesy."*

Everything that we do has to be done because we love God, and we love our brother and sister in the Lord. That's why we serve the Lord. That's why we act the way we do as believers. That's why we're not ashamed to be an expressive church. We should want to please God more than we want to please man, so we're not ashamed to step out and dance, because dancing is one way God's Word tells us to worship Him. Even if others in church don't dance, we should be obedient to His Word.

Revelation 19:10 says that Jesus is the Spirit of prophecy. In Joel 2:28, referring to the day of Pentecost (Acts 2:14-18), it says that your sons and your daughters (everybody) will prophesy, dream dreams, and see visions. You will notice that it doesn't say every now and then within several generations someone might prophesy. It says,

> *"And it shall come to pass afterward,*
> *That I will pour out My Spirit on ALL*
> *flesh;*

> *Your sons and your daughters shall*
> *prophesy,*
> *Your old men shall dream dreams,*
> *Your young men will see visions. And*
> *also on My menservants and on My*
> *maidservants*
> *I will pour out My Spirit in those*
> *days."*

Everybody is going to prophesy. Is that what the Bible says? Yes! We just read in I Corinthians 14 that **we should desire to prophesy.** So we see that there is a spirit of prophecy <u>in the beginning</u>, within the foundation.

<u>VISITATION VS. HABITATION</u>

> *"Now therefore, you are no longer*
> *strangers and foreigners, but fellow*
> *citizens with the saints and members of*
> *the household of God,*
> *having been built on the foundation*
> *of the apostles and prophets, Jesus Christ*
> *Himself being the chief cornerstone.*
> *In whom the whole building, being*
> *fitted together, grows into a holy temple*
> *in the Lord,*

> *in whom you also are being built together for a dwelling place of God in the Spirit." (Ephesians 2:19-22)*

Verse 22 says *you are being built together for a dwelling place.* Most people enjoy ministry gifts who visit their church, but they are not very fond of ministry gifts who "habitate." It's all right if the ministry gift comes for a visit, or if a revival comes through town, hits hard, and maybe exposes a little sin. However, if this goes on for any length of time, people often feel infringed upon. Their flesh grows weary and much too uncomfortable for their preference.

Apostles and prophets are anointed to see what goes on in the spirit realm. So when an apostle or prophet comes into the church, they will begin seeing, and exposing things that are not right or out of order. They start dealing with these things by uprooting, replanting, and pulling unrighteous strongholds. This is when it gets a little uncomfortable, and the idea of a visiting preacher is much more welcomed than one who "habitates."

WHO CAN PROPHESY?

In the New Testament pattern, corporate prophecy was administered by elders, a presbytery, or by an individual with a five-fold gifting. These people were

<u>called bishops or overseers, which meant they resided over a church.</u>

In the New Testament there were apostles who pastored churches, prophets who pastored churches, and evangelists who were over churches as well. They were also called bishops or overseers. This is something that I will address as we go on, because this has become a foreign concept to the body of Christ.

Any one of these offices could and should move prophetically. We should be a prophetic people. It is something that God desires to bring back into the Body. We've heard so many sermons about being a prophetic people, and have been excited about every one of them. However, **being a prophetic people means that we understand and operate in a prophetic anointing.** We should not only get the direct word of the Lord and have it confirmed by others, but we should also be able to come together as a church body and have our questions answered and our needs met by the Spirit of God.

The Bible gives accountability for everything it commands or provides. It makes it plain that when someone prophesies, that others are to stand by and listen and judge the prophecy.

This even goes for when someone calls you on the phone and says, "I have a word from God for you." Listen to the word. If you need to call somebody for the confirmation or wise counsel, then call somebody. Call the pastor, call an elder, call someone else that you know who is sensitive prophetically and sensitive to the word of the Lord. If you feel a check in your spirit, you look to godly counsel to confirm it. They may say to you, "Yes, they're right, and you need to deal with that." Or, "Yes, you're right, that is a direction that God wants you to go in." That is the way it is supposed to happen.

The Bible says to "covet earnestly" the prophetic, which means to "desire firmly" or "to lust for," in the Greek. Earnest desire is an inner longing. You must inwardly long to prophesy. By doing this, you will bring the spirit of prophecy into your life and church. It is imperative that we do this.

Wherever prophecy is not a regular function of the church, there is (1) confusion, (2) a lack of spiritual gifts, and (3) a lack of assured victory in people's lives. Its always available, and it always will be. The Bible says that all of us are to prophesy at some level.

WHAT ACTIVATES PROPHECY?

"'Let us be glad and rejoice and give Him glory, for the marriage of the Lamb is come, and His wife has made herself ready.'

And to her it was granted to be arrayed in fine linen, clean and bright,

> ***for the fine linen is the righteous acts of the saints.***
>
> ***Then he said to me, 'Write: Blessed are those who are called to the marriage supper of the Lamb!' And he said to me, 'These are true sayings of God!***
>
> ***I fell at his feet to worship him, but he said to me, 'See that you do not do that! I am your fellow servant, and of your brethren, <u>who have the testimony of Jesus.</u>***
>
> <u>***Worship God! For the testimony of Jesus is the spirit of prophecy.'"***</u> ***(Revelation 19:7-10)***

The anointing to prophesy comes with worship. **Worship activates a prophetic utterance.** Your spiritual ears begin to hear, your spiritual eyes begin to open, and you can see things because you are tuned in to look for them. Its not a matter of how long you have been in Christ, anyone can flow in prophecy. There are questions that many people need answered at various times in their life, and **God intended for the prophetic to flow on a regular basis.** Once you begin to learn it, and be trained to it, then you can move in it on your own, in your own worship time. Worshipping God pulls answers from heaven into your being. It pulls peace into your being. **You will never get very far in the prophetic realm if you're limited in worshipping**

God. That's why people usually don't have trouble praising God, but you will notice that whenever a church switches from praise to worship, a line is drawn through the congregation. People who are not accustomed to being intimate with the Spirit of God, are usually confused, weary, troubled, and ready to sit down. It is in that place of worship that the spirit of prophecy can bring necessary things into your life.

You can do this yourself. You can usher these things into your spirit by worshipping God. How do you do this? You give yourself to God in your worship.

Your level of worship determines the degree or the strength of the spirit of prophecy in your own life. <u>Prophecy is the word of the Lord bubbling up on the inside of you.</u> This word will give you direction for your life. People who know how to worship God will often have a strong prophetic anointing about them.

Worshipping the Lord develops your capacity for the prophetic anointing to fill your insides, so you don't walk around wondering what the will of the Lord is for your life. Worship draws a line through surface Christianity and true spiritual hunger.

Prophecy shows you the direction of God, and the will of God. When you flow prophetically, you know the will of God. This is the blessing of being a prophetic people, you're not a wanderer.

The level of knowing God's divine will and purpose for the majority of our lives is not known,

because the operation of prophecy and the prophetic anointing is missing from the majority of people's lives. There is little understanding of it and therefore many do not receive it.

THE DOOR OF INCREASE

While everyone can operate in prophecy and should move in a level of prophetic utterance, there are various levels of authority.

> *"not boasting of things beyond measure, that is, in another man's labors, but having hope, that as your faith is increased, <u>we shall be greatly enlarged by you in our sphere,</u>*
>
> *to preach the gospel in the regions beyond you, and not to boast in another man's sphere of accomplishments.*
>
> *But 'he who glories, let him glory in the Lord.'*
>
> *For not he who commends himself is approved, but whom the Lord commends." (II Corinthians 10:15-18)*

In this passage, the apostle Paul is giving a strategy for increasing the authority of Christ in us personally.

A lot of times we think if we can move up in title or if we can get more responsibility, we will increase. But the method established by God is really plain and simple. **It comes through stewardship.**

Paul is saying in this passage that his level of authority, or sphere of influence and rule, is increased by his ability to impart what he has inside of him to another. His increase is not because he's trying to usurp his authority, but because he is taking his faith and transferring it to another person.

You must **first respond properly** and faithfully with the authority level God gives you before you will receive more. Every one of us has been given a certain group of people with whom we associate, and that circle of people is our sphere of influence.

How much faith in Jesus Christ, the blessings of God, and the kingdom of God, are you imparting into your sphere of associations? Many of us can only handle two or three people within our sphere in the beginning. However, we want to go beyond that into greater responsibility. There are others of us who just seem to readily and radically love people, love God, and share our faith freely. These are the ones who grow and increase the fastest in their sphere of authority. **By loving people and imparting your faith, doors open for you and blessings come into your life.**

You must exercise stewardship over what you have been entrusted with. In the book of Matthew, Jesus told the parable of the talents. When the master came back, He was looking for the servant who multiplied the talent. The problem is that some people don't want to talk about or be held accountable for what's been given to them.

Your ability to take your faith and impart it into another person actually establishes you in the faith. **Establish another, and you will become established.** That's a principle of the Word of God.

A lot of people say, "Well, you know, it's wrong to want gifts. If God wants to give it to you, He'll give it to you."

The Bible says to desire gifts. Why? **Because Jesus died so you could have them. Those who desire them, get them. That's why churches who don't preach about the gifts of the Spirit, churches who don't go after them, churches who don't pray for them, don't get them.** I Corinthians 14:39 says, *"Desire earnestly to prophesy and do not forbid to speak with tongues."*

Why do churches forbid it? To put it bluntly, for many, it is because they are disobedient and rebellious to the scriptures and the ways or methods of heaven.

I Thessalonians 5:20 says, *"Do not despise prophecies."* The 26 Translation Version of the Bible says, *"Don't despise prophetic utterances, don't despise those who desire to prophesy, don't despise those who give out prophetic utterances, don't despise those who have prophetic giftings, don't despise those kind."*

Even if you've seen the gift be used in the wrong way, spiritual gifts should not be shut down. There's a way to do it and follow proper Biblical order. The Bible says, *"Test all things, hold fast what is good."* (I Thessalonians 5:21)

> *"You are My battle axe and weapons of war:*
> *For with you I will break the nation in pieces;*
> *With you I will destroy kingdoms;*
> *With you I will break in pieces the horse and its rider;*
> *With you I will break in pieces the chariot and its rider;*
> *With you also I will break in pieces man and woman;*
> *With you I will break in pieces old and young:*
> *With you I will break in pieces the young man and the maiden;*
> *With you also I will break in pieces the shepherd and his flock;*
> *With you I will break in pieces the farmer and his yoke of oxen;*
> *And with you I will break in pieces governors and rulers."*
> *(Jeremiah 51:20-23)*

Also, Jeremiah 1:10 speaks of the basic overall function of the prophetic, which is to root out, to pull down, to destroy, to throw down, to build, and to plant.

The prophetic anointing is sent by God to touch every single area of life. **Prophecy sets a course.** Paul told Timothy to wage a war according to prophecy. He told him again that the gift was given to him by prophecy.

The devil hates those churches and those people who flow in the Holy Spirit because these people aren't controlled, nor held back. They defeat the devil at every turn, destroying the works of the enemy, and manifesting Jesus.

Chapter 3

Pursuit - The Proof of Desire

"Pursue love, and desire spiritual gifts, but especially that you may prophesy." (I Corinthians 14:1)

The Lord spoke something to my heart not too long ago that caught me a little off guard, but it really sunk in as a revelation. He said to me, *"I gave My life to make gifts available to men."* And then He said it again in a different way, *"I gave My life to make prophecy available to the church."* This statement exploded in my spirit. But then He said, *"But you have to desire prophecy for it to work."* He then went on to remind me of the scriptures that talk about exercising the spiritual gifts, and I began to realize that this is where faith comes in. It involves our willingness to begin walking in the gifts of the Spirit. Most of us wait on some divine, sovereign act before we will even consider operating in spiritual gifts. However, scripture makes it very plain that we are to *desire* them.

When Jesus Christ ascended up into heaven, the Word says, *"He gave gifts unto man."* He sent them into the earth, but whether we receive them and operate in them is basically up to two things:

1. **The amount that we hunger after them.**
2. **The amount of exercise that we give them.**

How does this exercise work? Well, when you first exercise your physical body, you don't lie down on a workout bench, put 500 pounds on a bar, and bench press it off your chest. You have to pursue physical fitness and strength. The word *"pursue"* in I Corinthians 14:1 is defined: **to engage in or keep at an activity. That's called practice!** The definition of *"exercise"* is **an act of using something to maintain or increase a skill.** Practice! So, how do you get to the point where you can bench press 500 pounds? It only comes by practice and exercise!

<u>MOVING OUT IN SPIRITUAL GIFTS</u>

To move out in spiritual gifts, you need to understand that Jesus, through dying on the cross, gave the church gifts. These gifts are the nine gifts of the Spirit listed in I Corinthians 12.

I Corinthians 14:1 says, *"Pursue love and desire spiritual gifts, but especially that you may prophesy."*

If you are told to desire something, then it's a good idea to know what that thing is and what it entails. I Corinthians 12:7-10 says,

> *"But the manifestation of the Spirit is given to each one for the profit of all:*
> *for to one is given the word of wisdom through the Spirit, to another the word of knowledge through the same Spirit,*
> *to another faith by the same Spirit, to another gifts of healings by the same Spirit,*
> *to another the working of miracles, to another prophecy, to another discerning of spirits, to another different kinds of tongues, to another the interpretation of tongues."*

All of us, as believers, can operate and flow in these gifts as the need arises and as the Spirit wills.

However, some people have tendencies or preferences towards one gift more than another. For instance, let's go back to the example of working out. Some guys, when they go to the gym, only like to work their arms and their chest. But, then they have little bird legs because they don't like to work out that part of their body. The result is this big strong guy with these little bitsy legs. These guys figure that others will focus on their muscular arms or ripping chest, instead of their bird legs.

The same thing applies in the spirit realm. There are many people who become accustomed to particular operations of the Spirit, and are comfortable with only those. Maybe they feel like they have the ability to just encourage people supernaturally. For example, when they get around somebody who is hurting, they feel the compassion of the Lord, and they are able to speak a ministering word during someone's time of need. So, they begin exercising this gift because they enjoy the results they get when they exercise that particular spiritual gift.

It is very easy in the pursuit of one thing to neglect other things that are just as relevant to our lives. Where some people may flow well in one gift, they may feel inadequate or uncomfortable with the other eight. They are uncomfortable with the other gifts because they haven't exercised them in their lives. They like to stick with the thing that they look or feel the best in. Since their arms look the best, or their chest looks the best, every time they go to the gym that is all they work on.

The Bible says that we are to **earnestly desire spiritual gifts**. That means more than one. God wants us to be well balanced. He wants us to have symmetry in the spirit. This will create an equal balance in the body parts. As a result, there will be just as much work performed by the legs, as the arms, or by the stomach, as the chest. To make this point applicable, there will be an equal balance in the Body of Christ.

If you are trying to work a particular area in natural exercise, normally you give that area more attention. However, in spiritual matters, many of us are ignorant because we do just the opposite. We function in what we feel comfortable with because we don't want to be embarrassed. Normally, the reason people exercise is to change the way they look. The same principle applies in the spirit realm. **There needs to be an active pursuit of those gifts that are not commonly in operation in your life right now.** Just as your body will never change unless you exercise it, these spiritual matters will never change if you avoid them.

PROFIT AND LOSS

I Corinthians 14:6 says, *"But now, brethren, if I come to you speaking with tongues, what shall I profit you?"* Everything that God has, He wants you to profit or benefit from it. When you make a profit, it means that you have something left over, you have abundance. In some churches, people come in one way, and they leave the same way. Oftentimes, these are churches that forbid people to prophesy or manifest the gifts of the Spirit. This is such a loss.

Now, notice verse 26 of chapter 14, it instructs us that when we come together, *we should have a psalm, a teaching, a tongue, revelation, and an interpretation.* How does everyone come together with these things? It is the result of exercising the things of God in their life. They have become equipped.

Some people equip themselves stronger with prophetic singing. Other people equip themselves stronger with teaching. Other people equip themselves stronger in praying in other tongues and giving interpretations, and other people with revelation. All of us should be exercising ourselves in these particular areas of the gifts of the Spirit and in the flows of God, otherwise we are unfit.

"But what shall I profit you," meaning, it is a minister's goal, it is a church's goal, it is your goal to bring profit to other people's lives. What you give shall be given back to you.

Here is the difference. You can speak to someone out of your own head knowledge, you can speak to somebody out of your memory, you can speak to someone out of some scriptures that you remembered and learned when you were a kid, or in another church, or an old message that you heard. But when it is prompted by the Spirit of God, then you will speak to someone by the Spirit, and you will bring profit to them, which in turn brings profit to you.

I'm not talking about selfish motives, but rather a Biblical principle. *"Give and it shall be given unto you."* (Luke 6:38)

I Corinthians 14:6 says,

"But now, brethren, if I come to you speaking with tongues, what shall I profit you unless I speak to you either by revelation, by knowledge, by prophesying, or by teaching?"

"The gift of prophecy is declaring the heartbeat of God to His Church..."

Norman Robertson

PART II

The Prophetic in Action

Chapter 4

Levels of the Prophetic

THE BELIEVER'S ANOINTING

There are <u>three levels</u> to the prophetic anointing. **The first one is the believer's anointing**, as a Spirit filled believer. Notice that almost every time in the Bible when we read that **they received the baptism of the Holy Ghost and spoke with other tongues as the Spirit gave utterance, it also says that they began to prophesy.** They spoke with tongues and prophesied. It says it over, and over that they spoke with tongues <u>and</u> prophesied.

The word "prophesy" in the Old and New Testaments basically means the same thing. It means bubble up, and flow like a fountain; to boil over, to

gush, or to pour forth words, to speak forth the mind and the counsel of God.

No believer should be without the Spirit of prophecy in his or her life.

The scriptures tells us in I Corinthians 14:3 that, *"He who prophesies speaks edification, exhortation and comfort to men."* That means when you speak to someone, you don't just quote scriptures, but out of your insides you are giving prophetic utterances. This means that the Spirit of God begins to bubble up in you and you pour it forth by an act of your will to surrender to the Holy Spirit and give it out.

There are two ways you do this. **First**, by acquainting yourself with the kind of ministries that operate with a spirit of prophecy so you can pull on that anointing. **Secondly**, by stirring yourself up, because the Word says that **every believer is to prophesy.** So, that means every believer **can** prophesy. Every believer should be able to utter forth the words and counsel from the Spirit of God. Every one of us should speak **edification**, which means to strengthen; **exhortation**, which means to encourage; and **comfort**, which means to soothe or to heal.

That doesn't mean that you just walk up to someone and say something like, "Everything is going to be okay, honey, I know it's rough right now." That's one way to comfort, but it's not prophecy.

That's a common level that most believers encourage people on. It really has nothing to do with prophecy or the anointing bubbling up out of them. When we speak, when we give counsel, or when we exhort, we should have that spirit of prophecy to impart life into others.

My wife and I have found that some of our most powerful and effective conversations with one another come when we move by the gift of prophecy. It is then that the words we speak bring comfort. We choose to let what we say come by the Spirit, rather than arguing over who is right or wrong in the situation. Then, what we say will come by the Spirit. We end up coming to a quick agreement, because we both desire the anointing of God to give us counsel. It destroys the plans of the enemy to bring strife and division in our home and relationship.

When we begin to disagree, we just stop and say, "Wait a minute, let's walk the floor, let's begin to stir ourselves, and let's come back and talk about it later." We then pray for the Holy Spirit of counsel and might, the Spirit of comfort and encouragement, to come into the situation. When we come back together, we will find that the Spirit of God is in it, instead of pride and selfishness. There is a difference when you utter forth the oracles of God and giving your own opinion. My opinion means nothing in the spirit realm, because the Word of God is our standard of life.

THE GIFT OF PROPHECY

The **second level** of prophecy is found in I Corinthians 12:9-10, which is **the gift of prophecy.** The gift of prophecy flows as the Spirit wills in a service.

When prophecy is given out, don't make the mistake of assuming that it is always the gift of prophecy in operation. Sometimes it is. **The similarity between a believer prophesying, and the gift of prophecy is that both will strengthen, bring edification, exhortation and courage or comfort. The difference is at the second level, the gift of prophecy goes one step further.**

"But if all prophesy, and an unbeliever or an uninformed person comes in, he is convinced by all, he is convicted by all,

And thus the secrets of his heart are revealed:

and so falling down on his face, he will worship God and report that God is truly among you." (I Corinthians 14:24, 25)

Prophecy reveals the secrets of men's hearts for the purpose of repentance, and a boost towards continuing in God's will. Usually, the gift of prophecy will operate from a congregational stand point. Very few times is it going to be a rebuke at this particular level. Nowhere in the Bible, except in the **office** of a prophet, is rebuke administered in this way. Even in the New Testament all things are done to edify, exhort, and comfort. All levels are built on this foundation. This is the message of reconciliation.

The gift of prophecy is not necessarily when you give someone a personal word of rebuke for his or her life. Remember, that's more in the **office** of the prophet. **When someone gives out a rebuke where they have no place to do so, they will have no anointing to deliver the rebuke either.** They are probably just stirred in their soul, or they feel like they need to justify themselves. They may have gone to God, but instead of having a time of sincere prayer, they got all stirred up in their soul. While they were in this soulish state, they came to "give a word." **This is how offense, hurt and confusion come in to play.** That's what you call "giving a piece of your mind," and not a piece of the Spirit of God.

Accuracy in the spirit according to the Word is so important. There have been a lot of churches that have been really messed up and hurt by "wandering" prophets. These are people who float around and try to give someone a word everywhere they go, but never get submitted to any authority or local church. The Bible says to *"know those who labor among you."*

What if you are given a word from someone and you are not sure if it is accurate? That's okay. The Bible says to test every word. First, take it before God, put it on a shelf, and sit quietly with a good attitude. If it's right, God will confirm His word to you. Allow leadership to judge the word in order to assist in bringing clarity. If the word is not right, then don't hold unforgiveness against the person who gave you the word, just pray that the Lord will minister accuracy to them.

Maybe you are the one who gave a prophetic word and someone did not receive it; or, you are a minister and you gave a prophetic word while ministering somewhere, and the pastor did not receive it. What are you to do? The same principle applies to you. You can either leave the church, or take it back to God, put it on a shelf, and sit quietly with a good attitude until God moves to show the accuracy of His word in the situation. There are times when you give a prophetic utterance and it's not received, but that's not your concern. Your concern was only to deliver that word. In that case, if there's not a response, you better sit back and start praying for that person, because there may be judgment on its way. If judgment comes, it will come swiftly. However, **we are not to be haughty or threatening with the idea of judgment. Corrective prophecies must always be filtered through the Spirit of grace.**

> *"...which is the manifest evidence of the righteous judgment of God, that you may be counted worthy of the kingdom of God, from which you also suffer;*

> *since it is a righteous thing with God*
> *to repay with tribulation those who*
> *trouble you." (II Thessalonians 1:5,6)*

A lot of people mistakenly think they can just sit around in the church and get by with unbelief without taking everything that God says as being for them. What they don't understand is that they cannot continue to deny the workings of the Holy Spirit and think that they're going to experience the blessings of God. God only tolerates this type of behavior for so long. He will begin to send retribution and judgment (encouragement and reproof) into a church because of the denial and unbelief. God is longsuffering and full of mercy and, because He is a loving Father, He will use a variety of methods to get our attention and bring accuracy into our lives for His glory.

Remember that the times that the prophetic or the apostolic anointing comes are at the **beginning of things, at the transition of things, and at the ending of things**. The reason these anointings are sent at those particular times is to help a church get through the tough times like at the beginning, the end, or in a transition. The apostolic and prophetic anointings are breakthrough anointings, and we need these in our churches.

We as a church have to recognize the apostolic and the prophetic anointings. We have to understand that God gives it for a purpose. Unless we submit to it, yield to it, and allow it to operate, we will not be able to flourish or reproduce and progress in the things of God.

THE OFFICE OF THE PROPHET

Earlier we spoke of two of the levels of prophecy. **The third level of prophecy is the office of the prophet.** It is the highest level of prophecy.

> *"See, I have set you this day over the nations (natural dominions) and over the kingdoms (spiritual dominions)."* *(Jeremiah 1:10) (emphasis added.)*

There are **six purposes** for the basic functions of the office of the prophet.

First is **the destruction of Satan's kingdom**. A prophet cannot overlook it. A pastor has a little bit more mercy, and he can seem to overlook stuff, sometimes too much. That's why it's important for these offices to work together. A prophet is a "seer" and a pastor is a "gatherer." Both are needed.

Prophets can pastor, apostles can pastor, evangelists can be pastors, all the five fold ministry gifts can pastor. According to the New Testament, there were people that functioned as one of these but who also were pastoring a church. However, an important requirement is that you have to have grace and anointing, and be appointed by God to do it.

We have examples of apostles pastoring churches, or prophets pastoring churches. We have examples of evangelists pastoring churches. These office gifts should recognize that more is needed in the body than just one gift. Pastors should make sure that the congregation is exposed to, and imparted to, by all of the five fold gifts so as not to be lopsided or out of balance.

Speaking about the office of the prophet, their first purpose is for the destruction of Satan's kingdom, and the **second is <u>to establish the Kingdom of God.</u>** Prophets have a very low tolerance for evil. They are compelled to minister deliverance and bring truth. Matthew 15:13 says,

> *"But He answered them and said,*
> *'Every plant which My heavenly Father*
> *has not planted will be uprooted.'"*

By uprooting unrighteouness, the Kingdom of God is established.

Some prophets have an administration of deliverance, and their anointing lies heavier in deliverance than other areas. There are others that have a heavier anointing in the area of healing. There are variables to that, but as a whole, a prophet's tool, or their strength, is in their voice.

A prophet, or any ministry gift, must be strong and secure in the fact that the words they speak are from God and anointed by God. Resistance against those words must never be taken personal or in an insecure manner. **Your gift is not your identity**. Your identity is found in Christ alone.

The third purpose of the prophetic office is <u>to destroy the works of the devil</u>. II John 3:8 says that, *"Jesus came to destroy the works of the devil."* Not the works of the Lord, but only the works of the devil. When the Spirit of God establishes something, the works of the devil are destroyed. James 3:13 says,

> *"Who is wise and understanding among you? Let him show by good conduct that his works are done in the meekness of wisdom.*
> *But if you have bitter envy and self-seeking in your hearts, do not boast and lie against the truth."*

Selfish ambition in your heart produces lying against the truth, which is a work of the devil. The purpose of the prophetic office is to destroy the works of the devil.

> *"This wisdom does not descend from above, but is earthly, sensual and demonic.*

> ***For where envy and self-seeking
> exists, confusion and every evil thing are
> there. But the wisdom that is from above
> is first pure, then peaceable, gentle,
> willing to yield, full of mercy and good
> fruits, without partiality and without
> hypocrisy.***
>
> ***Now the fruit of righteousness is sown
> in peace by those who make peace."***
> ***(James 3:15-18)***

A prophet who compromises is going to be
judged by God for agreeing with the works of the devil,
instead of destroying them.

**The fourth purpose of the prophetic office is
to throw down.** Jeremiah 31:28 talks about throwing
down the altars of the heathens. The prophetic may
encounter rebellion or control, or witchcraft and pride
without even knowing anything in the natural. Prophetic
preaching seems to operate with a type of tracer for
things which are out of order or of the devil. Someone
might try to hide behind a loud "amen," but the prophet
still feels it, and his or her anointed preaching continues
to expose it.

This is yet another reason why a pastor has to
have the prophetic office come in and out of his church.

The prophetic anointing hits areas of sin and
rebellion under the obedience of the Spirit of God. Even
though it comes across in a personal manner, it's not

individually directed at anyone. This really bothered me a lot in my early days because every time I would preach under this anointing, somebody would say to me, "You said that about me." However, that's when you should be secure in the message from God and not be insecure about the response. Always encourage with scripture and a loving heart.

The prophet also pulls down. II Corinthians 10:4 speaks about *pulling down strongholds*. We see that the prophetic is confrontational, and even pronounces judgment at times. They uproot spirits from dwelling places through prophetic utterances. The focus is never on people, but the demonic spirits operating in or through a person or territory.

The **fifth and sixth purposes of the prophetic office are good things. <u>They build up after they remove, and then they plant the Word of God in your heart.</u>** Prophets have been hated by the devil for centuries; nevertheless, accurate prophets have a genuine love and compassion for people. They have a hatred for the devil and his works, but they have a genuine compassion for people.

Let me demonstrate these six purposes through a personal testimony.

When I first came to the area where I live and have a church, I did my best to come with just a pastoral attitude, and be a good pastor. But there was a problem! I was getting beat up by the devil. I asked the Lord why this was happening, what was going on? And He said to me, *"You don't start a church without the prophetic and the apostolic operations. It's here for you, but you've got to yield to it."*

I was thinking, "Oh God, I don't want to, I don't want to rock the boat."

And God said, *"No, there is a need for these operations to come in."* He told me that there were two reasons. **(1)** He said, *"I have ought against this area."* **(2)** He said, *"The area cannot be broken open spiritually without the prophetic and apostolic."* The specific words the Lord gave me were this, *"There's a conspiracy in the land."* As I prayed that's all I heard over and over. I acknowledged that I heard what He said, but I didn't know what He wanted me to do.

"Conspiracy" means to join in a secret agreement to do an unlawful or wrongful act, and to use such means to accomplish a lawful end. In other words, it looks good on the outside, but there are undermining works that are producing unrighteouness and false religion. This was a major problem in the area where I live.

The Lord also gave me a prophecy in the beginning days of planting my church. He said this:

> *"I've sent you, even as Jonah, to come, to warn, and to encourage. The church has allowed much to take place in this area because they have forsaken their divine purpose. There are conspiracies and things being done in the heavenlies to*

make this area a spiritual stronghold, a gate of hell. New Age has gone unchallenged. Indian mysticism has gone unchallenged. This area is declared by satanic spirits as a launching point to take over a region, to be a doorway of evil spirits. So I have sent, and am sending voices to be an alarm against this evil work, and to awaken My people out of slumber and recognize their true spiritual condition. My grace, My weapons, My anointing will cause you to arise and take back this territory. Men, women, children and eternal destinies lie in the awakening of My people."

Through the prophetic anointing, I understood why there was such a heaviness in the area. I understood why, in the past, churches were unable to survive in this area. That's why the Lord began to speak to me through the prophetic anointing.

The Lord spoke to me out of Revelations 18:20, ***"Babylon hates the apostles and the prophets, and have murdered many of them."*** Babylon in the Bible is always representative of false religious systems.

The personal testimony I just gave was the beginning of freedom being brought to our church and our region through the six purposes and functions of the prophetic in operation.

Chapter 5

Teaching and Preaching with the Prophetic Anointing

The Bible tells us that there are discerning of spirits, words of wisdom, words of knowledge, faith, the gifts of healing, prophecy, the working of miracles, different kinds of tongues, and interpretation of tongues. In I Corinthians 14:1 it says, *"Pursue love, desire spiritual gifts, especially that you might prophesy."*

The church is about to enter a time where there will be a lot of people who move in what I call the prophetic preach, or the prophetic teach. Over the last several years the Body of Christ, has been experiencing a restoration. There was a season when the pastoral gift was restored to the Body. Similarly, the office of the evangelist and teacher were emphasized during particular seasons of restoration.

The church went into a great teaching time in the 80's. This is when foundational books began to be written and the church was exposed constantly to the gift of teaching. But when the prophetic movement came on the scene after this season, many churches didn't want to receive it because they were stuck in the season of teaching.

What they failed to realize is, while there are still teachers, there are different types of teaching. One of the things that we need to understand is that when each season changes, the five-fold ministry, which is the evangelist, the prophet, the apostle, the pastor, the teacher, all take on a different type of flair or administration. They are still individual in their giftings, but when God begins to emphasize a particular area it affects everybody. For instance, when God sends an emphasis on intercession, everybody, whether apostle, prophet, evangelist, pastor, or teacher, will begin to intercede. This happened when a man named Larry Lea moved strong around the nation with the call to commit to one hour of prayer. This was an emphasis of God. I believe that during this time, God was trying to stretch all of our weak prayer lives into something that was more meaningful.

The prophetic teach ministers more by inspiration than it does by outline. The prophetic teacher is someone who studies to show himself approved. He or she gets full of the Word of God, full of the Spirit of God, then they get in their prayer closet before they minister and wait until they are endued with power from on high. They have the Word and the Spirit in them.

Jesus was a prophetic preacher. When he preached the Sermon on the Mount it wasn't from an outline on something He had preached before. Instead, he sat down, He saw the people, he felt their needs, and then he began to minister according to what was going on in the atmosphere. The prophetic deals with the now, and nails it down.

REVEALS, DEALS, DISCERNS, EXPOSES

1.   **Prophetic preaching/teaching reveals the heart of God.** It reveals what God is doing now. It shows what God did in the past, what He's doing now, and where it's leading in the future. In His preaching, Jesus didn't beat around the bush or generalize. He used illustrations that the people could relate to. When He talked to fishermen, He gave them fishing illustrations. This is the same way a prophetic preacher ministers today. And that is why people say, "Well, you know, I feel like he's preaching right at me." This is a good thing. It means that the Holy Ghost is doing His job. He's hitting right where it needs to be hit. He's dealing with what needs to be dealt with.

Prophetic preaching and teaching reveals Heaven's word, Heaven's will and purpose, not in a general way but intensely and thoroughly.

There are two kinds of people that prophetic ministry reaches. <u>Those that it bothers, and those that it blesses.</u>

It bothers those who are hiding behind sin, flesh, wrong doctrines, personal preferences, or strongholds. Prophetic preaching doesn't just give you something nice and fancy that can appeal to your head just so that you can still hold a bunch of junk in your heart and never have it dealt with or exposed. When prophetic preaching comes out, it deals with those things.

2.   **Prophetic preaching/teaching does not bring condemnation, but conviction.** Condemnation pinpoints something and gives guilt without hope. Conviction pinpoints something and shows you a way out. Hope is always associated with conviction.

The other type of people that prophetic preaching and teaching reaches are those who are blessed by it. These are those people with pure hearts and pure motives. It blesses those who are tenderhearted and teachable.

3.   **Prophetic preaching/teaching blesses those who desire change in their life, not people who are stuck.** When prophetic teaching begins to go out, it confirms things that the Holy Spirit has already

been speaking to people. On the other hand, churches where the people are full of carnality and worldliness are set in their ways and don't want to change. Prophetic teaching will probably only irritate them, rather than bring change or confirmation.

4.   Prophetic preaching deals with the heart of the people to set them free. Usually when someone goes into a prophetic church for the first time, they feel uncomfortable. (True peace is peace with God, not quiet singing with birds chirping. **True peace is not soulishly attained, it comes from being divinely aligned with God.** Peace is living by God's Word, God's will, and God's ways.) This is because everything inside of them is being challenged to change. True motives and intents of the heart are exposed. Prophetic preaching reveals the heart of man. It hits square in the eyes, the inner wrongs of people, exposing and uprooting them.

5.   Prophetic preaching discerns an atmosphere. It recognizes and it confronts territorial strongholds. It has an ability to see into the atmosphere of a place. Prophetic preachers know that if they don't track an atmosphere and pull down opposing forces, that those opposing forces will come in and try to steal the anointing out of the room. This is because it is an anti-Christ spirit. Christ means the "anointed One." These spirits are anti-anointing. They (demonic forces) come in to defy the anointing, to blaspheme it, to speak against it, to hold high-mindedness against it. They work to bring destructive thoughts, attitudes, and actions into a service.

The prophetic anointing is like a watch dog when it comes in to a room. The dog hears a sound that's not right and begins to growl. The spirit of prophecy in a church reveals the heart of God, it reveals the heart of man, and it discerns atmospheres. The spirit of prophecy looks into the atmosphere and sees the things that are out there. It feels things flying around in the room, and it begins to peg and nail those things down. However, the people still have a choice to either receive what the prophetic is saying or rise into rebellion, making a stand against God and what He is saying. When the ministry of the Word goes out, it is to help people grow, and change, be edified, be encouraged, be filled, and go on to new levels and new places in God.

6. **Prophetic preaching exposes the enemy for who he is.** It flushes him out, it chases him down, and defeats him. Evil and flesh cannot hide, not even behind a religious mask. That is why the prophetic often seems to aggravate, especially in cases of hidden sin.

7. **Prophetic preaching makes declarations, calling things that be not as though they were.** These declarations are not words given to an individual, but declared over an entire church, over an entire territory or atmosphere. This strong preaching opens the heavens through prophetic declarations and faith.

8.   Prophetic preaching/teaching keeps you free and spiritually healthy. There is a freshness in this type of preaching. It always seems to come across fresh; even if it is something you've heard preached a million times before.

In Acts 16:17, a girl followed Paul and cried out saying, *"These men are servants of the Most High God, who proclaim to us the way of salvation."* If prophetic preaching is going out correctly, someone is going to get mad, and someone is going to get blessed. Somebody is going to get convicted, and somebody is going to become a convict in their heart against God and the things of God. They'll be aggravated at it and they won't like it, but its purpose is to keep and maintain spiritual fitness. When bondages are broken in an atmosphere, as well as in personal lives through prophetic preaching, freedom will be evident.

"A prophet does not always take a systematic approach to teaching and preaching. He may jump back and forth as he preaches under prophetic inspiration. He sees different things, and this can express itself in a variety of ways."

Ulf Ekman

"Today we are seeing the growth of a major restorational movement throughout the church: the prophetic movement."

Dr. Bill Hamon

PART III

Reforming & Restoring

Chapter 6

Prophetic Building

In this chapter I'm going to talk about working on a building. All of us are at different places in our lives. We are all **"building"** something in our own individual lives. We are also building something corporately as the Body of Christ.

It is easy to think about building, to get ideas about building, or to look at house plans. It's easy to shout about the words of Jesus, about the building of the church, and the gates of hell not prevailing against it. **We get excited about Jesus defeating death, hell and the grave on the cross. However, we have to "build" these things into our lives.** A church has to build the things of God into an area. This is where the work of God begins. It is here we need to decide and determine what is of God, and what is of man.

A church should not build on the ideas of a people or the culture of a people, because these things are what the Bible called wood, hay and stubble. **A church should not be built on the ideas and opinions of man, and what man thinks a church should be.** Nor should a church operate on private opinions of how the people in a church should act, how everyone should be treated, or how everyone should worship. All of these things are clearly defined for us in the scriptures. **The Bible outlines how our lives and the church are supposed to be built, and the way both should function.**

If God, through Jesus Christ, gave us all the authority that we need to overcome, to be empowered, to heal the sick, to cast out devils, and to speak with other tongues as the Spirit of God gives utterance, then we have both the right, and the ability to build correctly.

When you mix the mortar for the foundations of your building it must be free from rocks and other foreign substances. We must get these hindrances out so that our foundation can be strong and free of debris. Many times, when we have weak or wrong foundations in our lives, there must come a reforming to what has been formed incorrectly. This reforming should happen from day to day, as we come into a greater development of the things of the Lord. **We have to allow God to come in to our lives and reform what has been formed wrongly. The devil hates the process of reformation and he tries to make sure that others hate it as well. God is in the process of restoring.**

We have been restored, and we are being further restored. We have been reformed, but yet we are still in the process of reformation in our lives. We are all continuing to be formed stronger, more completely, to the image of Jesus Christ. The day that you quit being reformed, and being pliable, is the day you open the door of your life to the devil.

God has given you authority. But you have an adversary, the devil, who walks about as a roaring lion looking for ways to get to you, to see that the reformation and restoration process is incomplete (James 5:8).

Prophetic building requires the exercising of authority in your life both from you and towards you.

Authority is never given for destruction. It is always given for edification. Edification means building up or strengthening.

> *"For even if I should boast somewhat more about our authority, which the Lord gave us for edification and not for your destruction, I shall not be ashamed."*
> *(II Corinthians 10:8)*

Some people think edification just means patting you on the back, rubbing your head and saying it's going to be all right, but **the word "edification" actually means to build.** It means to strengthen. Sometimes people don't like true biblical edification. Instead they want somebody to sing them a love song, but Paul said that edification comes to build something in you.

Most people don't like to have something built in them, because to have something built in you means something else has to be torn down.

Paul said that he was not ashamed of this, though he goes on to say that his bodily presence is weak and his speech contemptible, but his letters were weighty and powerful.

There are two main things that <u>prophetic building</u> does.

1. **<u>It builds an altar, or a relationship with God.</u>** If you're going to remain with the spirit of prophecy, move with the spirit of prophecy, have the authority of the spirit of prophecy, you've got to maintain relationship with God.

2. The altar represented the **<u>preparation for the manifestation of the Spirit of God</u>**. Many times, simply by preparing yourself, you are enabled to have the manifestation and blessings of God poured out on your life.

ATTRIBUTES OF PROPHETIC BUILDING

The first attribute of prophetic building is called **prophetic proof** which we see in I Kings 18 verses 38 and 39.

Elijah commanded that a ditch would be dug all around the altar and that water would be poured in it. Flesh wasn't going to be able to perform this miracle. The Spirit of God was going to have to show up.

> *"Then the fire of the Lord fell and consumed the burnt sacrifice, and the wood and the stones and the dust, and it licked up the water that was in the trench.*
>
> *Now when all the people saw it, they fell on their faces; and they said, 'The Lord, He is God! The Lord, He is God!'"*

What's the point of this? Elijah had the authority to back up what he said. A lot of people do a lot of talking, but when it comes down to it, there isn't any fire.

Obviously, authority is not manifested in the way you look, how long you've been around, or what kind of title you have. **That's all nice, and that may mean something, but if you don't have substance to back up your title, you really have no respectable authority.**

This would be applicable to churches that always talk about the power of God, but never have any power of God demonstrated. It is in this case that questions should arise like, "Okay, so we believe in a healing Jesus, but when is somebody going to be healed?"

Verse 40 shows us another attribute which is **prophetic judgment.**

> *"And Elijah said to them, 'Seize the prophets of Baal! Do not let one of them escape!' So they seized them, and Elijah brought them down to the Brook Kishon, and executed them there."*

Prophetic judgment sees something wrong, cuts it off and stops it.

Sometimes, prophecy may come in a manner where someone says, "The Lord loves you, and He's going to open a door for you. He's had His hand on you, and He's seen your faithfulness, and He just blesses you, and wants you to know that His love is with you."

But then, as the authority level of the prophet increases, there may come a word like, "The Lord is about to open a door for you, and you've been faithful, but nevertheless the Lord says, if you make the wrong decision, this and this and this will surely befall you. So the Lord says this day, heed the voice of the Lord and do what He tells you."

There is a difference in the authority of each of those words. Prophetic judgment is able to back up what it says, is not controlling, is not witchcraft, is under authority, is not abusive, is not selfish. It is not self-centered or full of pride. It functions according to Biblical structure. There is a right place for prophetic judgment.

As prophetic and apostolic anointings come stronger in churches, one of the things that you'll see restored is various levels of prophetic judgment. That's scary to most people, but actually it's true. This is one of the characteristics of a prophetic church.

There are churches that have found themselves being challenged in an unrighteous way by those who hold office in the city. Prophetic warnings have gone out to those holding the positions, but they were not heeded. Then within several days time, those who held the positions lost their office. This is a prophetic judgment. Why does this happen? Because those people were standing in the face of God, defying the move and the progression of the gospel, and prophetic judgment displaced them.

Jezebel and the prophets of Baal massacred the prophets of the Lord, and when it comes down to massacring the true, there will be prophetic judgment that rises up to put a stop to it.

Prophetic judgment is not against people. It is not a personal war. Some people try to make

prophetic judgments out of their own offenses. That's not how it works.

Prophetic judgment is not a game of manipulation. Don't mess around with it. If you don't have a position of authority in the spirit, I'm not speaking of a title, (I'm speaking of a position of authority in the spirit realm, that is backed with plenty of proof,) don't mess around with it.

I Kings 18: 42-44 says,

> *"So Ahab went up to eat and drink. And Elijah went up to the top of Carmel; then he bowed down to the ground, and put his face between his knees,*
> *and said to his servant, 'Go up now, look toward the sea.' So he went up and looked and said, 'There is nothing.' And seven times he said, 'Go again.'*
> *Then it came to pass the seventh time, that he said, 'There is a cloud, as small as a man's hand, rising out of the sea!' So he said, 'Go up, say to Ahab, 'Prepare your chariot, and go down before the rain stops.'"*

This is an example of waging war with prophecy. This is also an attribute of prophetic building and what I call **prophetic praying**. **Prophetic praying births**

things. It births a move of God, it births an anointing, it births a call, it births miracles, and it births the promises of God into existence. It's not just your fly-by-night, make a confession about being a conqueror in Christ everyday. There's a place for that, but that's not the kind of praying that causes birthings to take place.

There is a need for prophetic praying to come back to churches. It needs to come back to individuals in their homes. If we call ourselves a prophetic people, in prophetic times, then prophetic prayer should be a normal part of our life, not just an occasional thing.

Elijah was birthing. He got down in a birthing position and groaned and travailed before God for the promise that was given. **Prophetic churches need to be churches of prophetic prayer and intercession.** Prophetic people need to be people of prophetic birthings and prophetic intercessions.

The devil has skillfully removed prophetic birthings out of the church, saying there is no need for prayer like that. That's how the church got into a "user friendly" mentality. That's why the church is now trying to please people instead of trying to please God. That's why some churches only allow people to speak in tongues in a special service or in the back room.

"And Ahab told Jezebel all that Elijah had done, also how he had executed all the prophets with the sword.

Then Jezebel sent a messenger to Elijah, saying, 'So let the gods do to me, and even more also, if I do not make your life as the life of one of them by tomorrow about this time.'

And when he saw that, he arose and ran for his life, and went to Beersheba, which belongs to Judah, and left his servant there." (I Kings 19:1)

Verse 4 says, *"But he himself went a day's journey into the wilderness..."* Notice that. Where did he go? The wilderness.

"...and came and sat down under a broom tree. And he prayed that he might die, and said, 'It is enough! Now, Lord take my life, for I am no better than my fathers!'"

He had just had the greatest victory in his life, and now he is in fear and ready to give up. Until we leave this earth, the fact is that you've got to fight. There's no way out of it. The day that you stop fighting, you're going to want to die, and you're going to be full of self-pity like Elijah was.

I Timothy 1:18 instructs us to, **war according to the prophecies given unto you.** You have to make war according to prophetic unction. If you move into the prophetic, you've got to be ready to fight.

Don't try to live off the victory, live off of your relationship. Don't try to live off of the defeat, live off of the relationship in Jesus Christ. The victory, or the defeat, has nothing to do with your reaction. It's called consistency. When things are good, you're the same. When things are bad, you're the same. When things are going great, you're still praying. When things aren't going great, you still pray. When you've just been defeated, you still pray, love God and worship God. When you've just won the greatest victory, you still pray, love God, and worship Him.

Some people are so selfish that they live in a perpetual cycle of victory, defeat, victory, defeat, victory, defeat. When the words of life come to them, they're so wrapped in their own opinion, their own defeat, their own little world of self-pity, that they refuse the bread of the angels, they refuse encouragement from other believers, they refuse the signs that are going on around them. They are blinded.

It wasn't a devil, it wasn't Jezebel, it wasn't other people, it wasn't Elijah's circumstances. He himself was so overcome with his own self-pity he wouldn't listen to the counsel of the Lord. When self-pity, pride, and selfishness become bigger than God, His counsel or His confirmation, that is when God begins to transfer your mandate and anointings to other people.

In the latter part of verse 16 of I Kings 19 it says, *"Go anoint Elisha as prophet in your place."*

Does this mean Elijah wasn't a great man? No, he was a great man. Does this mean that God wasn't pleased with his past obedience? No, He was very pleased, because he was written of as a great man in the Bible.

Prophetic victory is won through consistency. If you don't remain consistent, you'll be an emotional wreck. You'll go from victory to defeat, victory to defeat, and victory to self-pity. You place yourself in a battle straight up against all the enemies of your life, and of your soul, and of your church and everything else. You must have stability and consistency. Basically you're saying, "I won't live in mediocrity, I will live all the way, and I will live in victory, and that's all there is to it." Consistency is your only key to victory.

Look at II Corinthians 10:11:

"Let such a person consider this, that what we are in word by letters when we are absent, such we will also be in deed when we are present."

The fact that you can talk a big talk is not enough. What really matters is that you have fruit in deed, in action, and substance.

"Now to Him who is able to establish you according to my gospel and the preaching of Jesus Christ, according to the revelation of the mystery kept secret since the world began

but now has been made manifest, and by the prophetic Scriptures has been made known to all nations, according to the commandment of the everlasting God, for obedience to the faith--" *(Romans 16:25-26)*

Chapter 7

Enemies of the Prophetic

Now that we have discussed the various levels and functions of the prophetic, it is also important that we identify the enemies of the prophetic. Remember that the definition of prophecy is the foretelling of the mysteries and will of God by divine inspiration; a forewarning, and the revealing of men's hearts to lead them to repentance. The devil hates this whole idea of Christians having the upperhand by the Spirit of God. We know that spiritual accuracy, progression and a greater revelation of Jesus Christ and His kingdom are just some of the benefits of prophecy. No wonder the devil has worked overtime for centuries to hinder God's people from flowing in this spiritual gift.

One of the most common tactics the devil uses is the operation of the spirit of Jezebel. I use the name

Jezebel only for illustrative purposes, using the characteristics of Queen Jezebel as seen in I Kings where she so viciously came against the prophets of God and Elijah. Let me state that this demonic spirit knows no gender, male or female. It can operate through whoever is willing to yield to its unrighteous behavior patterns. Lets look at some of these characteristics that attempt to silence the voice of the prophetic.

> *"And Ahab told Jezebel all that Elijah had done, also how he had executed all the prophets (of Baal) with the sword. Then Jezebel sent a message to Elijah, saying, 'So let the gods do to me, and more also, if I do not make your life as the life of one of them by tomorrow about this time.'"* (I Kings 19:1-2) (emphasis added)

1. This spirit loves to have power (self-idolatry - wants all the attention).
2. False prophetic, expresses selfish motives through prophecy which is otherwise known as divination (very mischievous and deceitful).
3. Abhors truth and God-ordained authority.
4. Always attracts emotionally needy, indecisive "Ahabs" (men or women).
5. Manipulative - uses sex or anything to work its own agenda.

6. Seducing (not only sexually)
    - Controls your mind.
    - Twists the truth.
    - Makes you doubtful and confused.
    - Flatters you.
    - Fights the works of repentance.

7. A murderer - wants to kill or abort the call of God over people's lives. (Jezebel hid the prophets of God in a cave, fed them bread and water and castrated them - took away their manhood or authority.)

8. Operates in witchcraft - controls the mind and will of another through spiritual manipulation which produces domination.

9. Gossips and slanders others, particularly those in leadership.

10. Very rebellious in several areas of his or her life.

11. Selfishly ambitious (wants position and notoriety).

12. Always exalts itself and enjoys intimidating others.

13. Hates repentance on a personal level, but likes to promote it corporately, because it loves legalism and likes to be the one who points out everyone else's sin.

14. Hates the prophets of God and the prophetic generation, because they come to bring repentance and reformation.

15. Uses others as its "mouthpiece" - like Ahab was to Jezebel.

16.   Avoids personal interaction with the body of Christ such as servanthood.
17.   Never has the joy of the Lord - always very serious in a "spiritual" sort of way.
18.   Belittles and attempts to disqualify others spiritually, promoting unworthiness.

10 CHARACTERISTICS OF FALSE PROPHETS

    Another enemy we should point out is the false prophet, which is the counterfeit of the true prophetic. The scripture warns us of false prophets and gives a pattern to judge them by. False prophets are identified by the following character traits:

1.   Pride and egotism.
2.   Arrogance.
3.   Boasting and exaggeration.
4.   Dishonesty.
5.   Covetousness.
6.   Rebellion - unwilling to submit to spiritual authority and often don't belong to a local church.
7.   Financial irresponsibility.
8.   Immorality
9.   Addictive appetites and habits.
10.   Confusion and disorder in the home.

These are all marks of a false prophet, according to scripture. It's a big mistake to let anyone get up and prophesy in your church that the leadership is not acquainted with, and who has not made an effort to bear some good fruit in the local church as well as in their personal life. It's likewise an even bigger mistake to allow someone you don't know, or that your pastor has not approved, to lay hands on you and prophesy. Its important that it is filtered through the leadership.

Here are some scriptures to study on the subject of how to recognize a false prophet.
- Matthew 7:15-23
- II Peter 2:1-3
- II Peter 2:10
- II Peter 2:12-19

These all describe a false prophet. Independent, unteachable, self-proclaimed prophets are dangerous. No prophet or believer should be allowed to prophesy unless they are submitted to a local church and pastoral oversight. **These guidelines will not be offensive to someone with a humble heart and the love of God operating through them towards the church and His people.**

Chapter 8

A Walk Through The Past

In the **1500's,** the Protestant movement came to the forefront with Martin Luther and his revelation of salvation by grace through faith alone.

In the **1600's,** evangelism, water baptism, and separation of church and state were emphasized. Why the separation of church and state? Because at that time, the church was running everything, but it was corrupt. Separation of church and state is actually the opposite of what most people believe it is. During that time, the church had so much power, but did not manifest the Spirit of Christ. Instead, it took the power, wealth, freedom, and authority it was blessed with and began dictating its own personal desires and agendas.

In the **1700's**, holiness, sanctification, and the setting apart of the church from the world were the emphasis. This was because the church needed a good cleaning after what it had been involved in up to that time.

In the **1800's**, faith healing and divine healing for the physical body was the main thrust. This was due to the fact that during the time of the restoration of holiness, people developed a mindset that true holiness involved an element of suffering. Therefore, man thought it was good to suffer. People began to think that you were more holy and acceptable to God if you had nothing, and that you would mean more to God if you were poor and broke. You were viewed as more holy if you were sick in your body, because then you were made strong in spirit. As a result, God began to send anointed ministers to heal people's sick bodies.

In the **1900's,** the Pentecostal experience, complete with the baptism of the Holy Spirit and speaking in other tongues, was the emphasis. The Pentecostal experience, like every move of God, covered all denominations. It is not a denominational manifestation. It covered every race; it is not a racial preference. It covered every culture; it is not a cultural way of life. It covered every background; it is not a background influence. It covers everything, because it is from God.

There was a long period in the **early 1900's** and the **1950's** when the church began to form a new government within itself. It began to organize itself, and denominations came to the forefront. That was the beginning of its end. As a matter of fact, the time that we are currently living in is being called by many people across the board, a "post-denominational period." This is because statistics show that a large number of people are leaving main line denominational churches, and even Pentecostal denominational churches. Even some of the charismatic churches that have become prominent are all of a sudden losing people because people always "follow the cloud." ***"Those who are led by the Spirit of God, these are the sons of God." (Romans* 8:14)**

People who want God, follow the Spirit of God. They don't follow denominations or a certain people group just because they happen to be a part of that group. For example, they don't follow the Hispanic culture just because they're Hispanic, or they don't follow the Russian culture just because they happen to be Russian. They know that when things begin to lose their life, and when people are resistant to the things of God, then God will begin to look for a people who will manifest what He's doing in the earth now. In the meantime, the people who carried the last move become the critics of the next move. The church faces opposition in attempting to build, especially after God has moved on to something new.

In the **1950's**, we had the **"Latter Rain Movement,"** which operated with a prophetic presbytery. This was a time when elders of the church focused heavily on fasting and praying to ordain people and release them into ministry. This function of a prophetic presbytery was returned to the church during this movement. Prophetic presbytery was a common occurrence in the New Testament.

> *"Do not neglect the gift that is in you, which was given to you by prophecy with the laying on of the hands of the presbytery.*
> *Meditate on these things; give yourself entirely to them, that your progress may be evident to all.*
> *Take heed to yourself and to the doctrine. Continue in them, for in doing this you will save both yourself and those who hear you." (I Timothy 4:14-16)*

During this time of prophetic presbytery, spontaneous praise and worship was brought back into the church. In the Bible, the majority of the time when people worshipped God, they worshipped spontaneously. This was a time when people were sensitive to the Spirit of God. When the spirit of praise would come in, people would begin praising with everyone joining in. The same thing happens with worship. All of a sudden the spirit of worship would come into the room, the people of God heard it, felt it, saw it in the spirit, and they responded to it by worshipping God from their spirits.

This is called being led by the Spirit of God. It is what keeps our lives from being a life of works only. God sent His Holy Spirit to lead us, teach us, and guide us into all truth. So if He did that, then that means that in everything that we do and say He wants to send supernatural directives into our lives. This is so we will know how to live, how to respond, and how to activate ourselves according to what the Spirit of God is bringing into our lives, or into a room, or into a church service.

In the **1960's**, there came the **"Charismatic Movement."** During the Charismatic movement, everything God did was predominantly sovereign. The people didn't have to work for what they received, it was handed to them on a silver platter. This movement brought about the renewal of all restored truth as seen in past movements to date.

In the **1970's**, there was the **"Word of Faith Movement."** During the Word of Faith movement, faith to believe God for "things" was emphasized because of some faulty teaching during the Charismatic Movement. But then God began to deal with His people on the principles of faith and how to operate within their covenant rights. God began to work with people on the level of their confessions even when they didn't feel any sovereign grace. Of course, like man so often does, many took this principle to an extreme, but God still emphasized His Word.

At this time God also began focusing on the prosperity of the Church. People began to realize that they didn't have to be poor in order to be spiritual. God began to show His principles for tithes and offerings. His goal was to activate the people's faith, get their confession in line, stand on the Word of God, and bring them into prosperity. The problem was that most people stopped right there. If they made it to this point, they didn't go any further.

WHAT ABOUT THE PROPHETIC?

In the **1980's,** came the **"Prophetic Movement."** This is when the gifts of the Holy Spirit were emphasized. Ephesians 2:20 says that the church was built with Jesus as the chief cornerstone and that we were built on the foundations of the apostles and prophets. First Corinthians 3:9-13 informs us that we are God's building and that we should "take heed" how we build in it. We are being built for a habitation of God's Spirit.

Every time one of these movements came about there were **two things** that came with it:

1. A voice that prophesied about the next coming.
2. Someone who would bring it into existence.

These two things occurred when nobody knew what it was or how to do it because it was not the norm. This was done in spite of the people's response to the new move of God when they said, "Well what I have now works fine for me."

The prophets in the **1980's** began prophesying about today. They began saying, "There's coming a day when the prophetic emphasis will begin to wane. And as the prophetic emphasis begins to wane, the church will enter into apostolic times." Now the church is in fact entering into the time of the apostolic.

<u>CHANGE IS GOOD</u>

Restoration and reformation will bring change into our lives. Some individuals and churches have strongholds (preset ideas and traditions that limit their receptivity to certain moves of God). Many people build comfort zones and cannot be flexible when God wants to come in and bring change. For instance, there are still people today who don't believe in faith healing even though it was restored in the 1800's. That's a long time ago, yet there are churches today who are still fighting it because they are content with living in the 1500's. They stopped at salvation by grace, and that's where they remained.

There are still those people that have trouble with the Protestant Movement. They still think that there is some kind of spiritual significance to worshiping statues. They still think that if you kiss so many babies, and help so many sick people, that you can be a saint (which, by the way, is nowhere in the Bible). Some still think that there must be a mediator between God and man, even though the Bible says there is only one Mediator and His name is Jesus (1 Timothy 2:5). I am not against these people, but I am for absolute truth.

Truth is birthed into the earth at different intervals. It's not new truth, because the Bible says there's nothing new under the sun (Ecclesiastes 1:9). It is divine enlightenment of certain scripture texts, revelation knowledge of truths and practices that have not been properly understood and practiced since the early days of the church.

The primary function of the Charismatic movement was to bring a restoration of everything from the 1500's till now. It was a renewal of all restored truth.

It's funny how Pentecostals fought Charismatics because they believed that unless you got all sweaty while you preached, prayed and worshipped or yelled as loud as you could, that you weren't anointed. On the other hand, the Charismatics believed that unless you were humming "Kum-ba-yah" with a euphoric cloud around you, that you weren't anointed either.

Instead of taking the best of both expressions of worship and just following the Spirit, we as humans have a tendency to become stuck in personal preferences.

We get preference minded, not realizing that preference is a sin when it comes to resist the things of God. If it's your car, get whatever color you want. If it's your house, get whatever size you want. If it's your shoes, get whatever kind you want. But with the things of God, take what He gives at the times that He gives them.

The revelation of divine truth is what brings you to the knowledge of what is right and what is wrong. It is what will cause you to make a stand when someone comes against a biblical truth that has come alive in you. God intends for us to follow Him. He is looking for people who are hungry and who have a right spirit.

When God begins to shed light on a specific truth, you will see that truth from Genesis to Revelation. You will wonder how you could have overlooked it when God sends divine enlightenment on it. You will see it for what seems like the first time.

For example with healing, God healed in Genesis, Exodus, Leviticus, and Numbers, and so on. Healing is mentioned all through the scriptures, with such scriptures as *Isaiah 53:5, "...by His stripes we are healed,"* and Mark 16:18 *"...lay hands on the sick and they will recover."* People will still argue about healing, though when you experience the liberty and freedom found only in God, you'll never want to go back to bondage, no matter who offers it. Galatians 5:1 says,

"Stand fast therefore in the liberty by which Christ has made us free, and do

***not be entangled again with a yoke of
bondage."***

What is bondage? Bondage is anything that is
contrary to the Word and the will of God.

TODAY IS A NEW DAY

There are pastors today who know that God is
changing the focus of the church and that we're going
into something else. It is sad, though that there are a
large number of pastors who are clinging to what is
comfortable to them and to their church. They are afraid
that if they change directions and step into the new thing
that God is doing, people will leave their church. As a
result, these <u>fearful pastors don't preach a current word,
choosing instead to rehearse a past truth over and over
again.</u>

It needs to be noted that scriptures never become
irrelevant. **We simply need to take the previous truth
with us into the next move of God.** There will always
be people of God who are hungering for what God is
doing and saying now. Contained within the current Word
of God are new anointings, new understandings, a new
love for God, a new peace, a new joy, and new
demonstrations of God's Spirit in the earth.

It's a new time; it's a new day, so we need to

prepare for it. If you want the reality, the refreshing, the presence and the glory of God, I encourage you to pursue it. Look in the scriptures, search your heart, and look at history. Church history is the testimony and confirmation that you are proceeding in the right direction, even when other people express opinions to the contrary. Don't stay in the past, but take the treasures of revelations and the testimonies of yesterday and allow them to be confirmed to you today. Grow from faith to faith, glory to glory and strength to strength!

> *"Jesus said to them, "Have you understood all these things?" They said to Him, "Yes, Lord."*
> *Then He said to them, "Therefore every scribe instructed concerning <u>the kingdom heaven is like</u> a householder who brings out of his treasure things new and old.""* *(Matthew 13:52)*

Chapter 9

Set On A Course

Prophecy is another way that you can gain spiritual profit, spiritual growth, and more understanding in the things of God. Prophecy gives you pieces of the puzzle that God has designed for your life. **It sets your life on a course that has been predetermined by God.**

In I Corinthians chapter 9, Paul speaks of running the race and finishing his course. For every one of us there is a course that God has set for our lives. What is *"a course?"* **A course has a beginning and an end,** and there are specific landmarks in the middle of a course.

Prophecy brings light to the course that your life is supposed to operate on. Ephesians 2:2 says,

> *"...in which you once walked according to the course of this world,*

according to the prince of the power of the air, the spirit who now works in the sons of disobedience,"

The world has a course for your life and tries to get you on it by pulling you in the direction that it is already going.

The Spirit of God reveals His course for your life in four main ways:

1. By His written Word.
2. By revelation.
3. By knowledge.
4. By prophecy.

When you prophesy it sets a course. We need to stay *"established"* in present truth, which means that we have to be fit in areas that are necessary in order that we may run the course that God has planned for us. This word "established" means: consistent, grounded, firm, and unmovable.

"And you He made alive, who were dead in trespasses and sins," (Ephesians 2:1)

Before you became born again with the life of Jesus Christ, your spirit was dead and on its way to hell. It was bound up in trespasses and sins.

"In which you once walked according to the course of this world, according to the prince of the power of the air, the spirit who now works in the sons of disobedience,
among whom also we all once conducted ourselves in the lusts of our flesh, fulfilling the desires of the flesh and of the mind, and were by nature children of wrath, just as the others."
(Ephesians 2:2-3)

When we invited Jesus Christ to come into our heart, He made our spirit man alive and made it sensitive to spiritual things. This enables us to be able to move by revelation, by prophecy, by teaching, and by divine understanding.

This comes through the shed blood of Jesus Christ, the redemptive work He did on the cross; His death, His burial, and His resurrection.

"And I also say to you that you are Peter, and on this rock I will build my church, and the gates of Hades shall not prevail against it." (Matthew 16:18)

In this passage, Jesus referred to building on the rock of revelation. Jesus said that He would build on the revealed knowledge of who Christ is, what Christ is, and what He would be in our lives.

In Galatians 1:12, Paul speaks about his calling and the course that was set before him, ***"For I neither received it from man, nor was I taught it, but it came through the revelation of Jesus Christ."***

And in Galatians 2:2, Paul states, ***"I went up by revelation and communicated to them that gospel..."*** Throughout the scriptures you'll find that one of the ways you understand the course that God has laid before you is through revelation. **Revelation is supernaturally revealed knowledge.**

STANDARD EQUIPMENT

I Corinthians chapter 14:1 (a) says, ***"Pursue love and desire spiritual gifts."***

Now, the scriptures would not tell you to desire something you're not supposed to desire. If God didn't think that it was okay for you to desire spiritual gifts, He never would have put that command in His Word. There are weapons that God has given us that are standard equipment for Christian living, and spiritual gifts are included in those weapons.

If a Christian tries to go through life without the weapons of the gifts of the Spirit, he or she would be like a Marine who was dropped off in the middle of the desert without all of his equipment. This Marine would be foolish to say, "I think I'll be fine with only my boots, my hat, my shirt and my pants. I don't need all that other stuff. Besides, I was told once before that those **tools** and **weapons** aren't for today."

That Marine would look very ignorant in his hat, his boots, and clothes when everybody else in his company sets up camp, builds a fire, erects their tents, and begins to clean their weapons.

Notice though that there are people like this Marine who, if it starts raining, always come over and seek shelter from those who have the proper equipment and provisions.

For instance, in the area of healing, those who are sick will go to a church that operates in healing and say, "They won't pray for healing at our church, but I love the church. I don't want to leave there, but would you pray for my healing anyway?"

They come in while it's raining, but when the rain stops they run back out again. Why live that way when God has given you **tools**, **weapons**, and **equipment** to use? He gives it to everybody, to *"whosoever will."* Who can be saved? *"Whosoever will."* Who can have the baptism of the Holy Ghost? *"Whosoever will."* If you desire it, you can have it. If you hunger and thirst after righteousness, God will fill you with righteousness. If you hunger and thirst after the gifts of the Spirit, God will fill you with the gifts of the Spirit.

I Corinthians 14:39 says, ***"Therefore brethren, desire earnestly to prophesy..."*** Or, covet earnestly to prophesy.   God wants to bring the gift of prophecy into the Church in a stronger way.

STIRRING IT UP

In I Corinthians 14:5, Paul states that ***all should prophesy.*** This scripture just assumes that everybody embraces the ability to prophesy. This must mean that it's available to everyone to prophesy as the Spirit of the Lord gives utterance.

How do you begin doing that? By faith. What does faith take? Obedience.

This is why Paul wrote Timothy, and said, ***"...Stir up the gift of God that is within you..."*** (II Timothy 1:6)

You have to desire and stir up the things that are given to you freely by God. This is a must if you are going to begin to exercise yourself to bring profit to both your life and others.

As was discussed in previous chapters, there are different levels of prophecy. There is **first** a basic level which all believers can operate in that involves edification, exhortation and comfort. I Corinthians 14:3 says, *"But he who prophesies speaks edification, exhortation, and comfort to men."* There is a **second** level of prophecy which is discussed in I Corinthians 14:24-25, where it speaks of revealing the secrets of the heart. This is where God uses you to reveal the course that God has laid out for someone, when there is no way in the natural you could have known such a thing. At this level, the secrets of the heart, the deep things in the recesses of another's being, are revealed.

We need to earnestly desire to prophesy so that we can profit in the things of God and be established in the work and the Word of the Lord.

We must bring the course of the Word of the Lord and the prophetic into our churches in a greater dimension. We need to stir ourselves up to step out in faith and exercise ourselves to prophesy.

"How is it then, brethren? Whenever you come together, each of you has a psalm, has a teaching, has a tongue, has a revelation, has an interpretation. Let all things be done for edification." (I Corinthians 14:26)

A PROPHETIC PEOPLE

Prophetic people know:

1. What God is doing.
2. What God is saying.
3. What God is expecting.

There are people who read the Bible every day and they're still confused. Many times it is because there is no prophetic word going forth in their life.

Corporate prophecy, as well as personal prophecy, gives specific direction to our lives.

II Peter 1:19-21 says,

"And so we have the prophetic word confirmed, which you do well to heed as a light that shines in a dark place, until the day dawns and the morning star rises in your hearts;

knowing this first, that no prophecy of Scripture is of any private interpretation,

for prophecy never came by the will of man, but holy men of God spoke as they were moved by the Holy Spirit."

Verse 20 is my focus, *"knowing this first that no prophecy of Scripture is of any private interpretation..."* The Bible makes it very plain in several passages that prophetic words are not enough unless they are confirmed, especially if they have something to do with other people's lives.

You can abort your own prophecy. You can delay your own prophecy. When God gives you a prophecy He gives it to you expecting you to be obedient to it.

However, the majority of people don't respond in obedience. As a matter of fact, some people get a word from the Lord and:

1.   They don't do anything about it.
2.   They mix it with their own agenda.
3.   They just wait around for it to come to pass.

On the contrary, the apostle Paul made it clear that you have to war according to your prophecy. In I Timothy 1:18, he said *"to wage war according to the prophecies that were previously given unto you."*

The prophetic word will never disagree with scripture, nor will it disagree with basic principles of common sense.

Is it okay for me to desire spiritual gifts? Is it okay for me to desire to prophesy? I Corinthians 14:1 says, *"Pursue love and desire spiritual gifts, but especially that you may prophesy."*

Many people are miserable because they don't have specific direction from prophetic utterance, and they spend years wandering around. There must come a respect and an earnest desire for the prophetic word in all of our lives.

In the Amplified translation of I Corinthians 14:24-26 (a) it says,

> *"But if all prophesy, (giving inspired testimony and interpreting the divine*

will and purpose) and an unbeliever or untaught outsider comes in, he is told of his sin and reproved and convicted and convinced by all, and his defects and needs are examined (estimated, determined) and he is called to account by all.

The secrets of his heart are laid bare; and so, falling on (his) face, he will worship God, declaring that God is among you in very truth.

What then brethren, (is the right course?)"

Then it goes on to say that when we come together, each one of us should have something spiritual to give to one another. That's what I'm going to focus on here.

Now look at I Corinthians 14: 29-33 (Amplified):

"So let two or three prophets speak (those inspired to preach or teach), while the rest pay attention and weigh and discern what is said.

But if an inspired revelation comes to another who is sitting by, then let the first one be silent.

For in this way you can give testimony, (prophesying and thus

*interpreting the divine will and purpose)
one by one, so that all may be instructed
and all may be stimulated and
encouraged;*

*For the spirits of the prophets, (the
speakers in tongues) are under the
speaker's control (and subject to being
silenced as may be necessary),*

*For He (Who is the source of their
prophesying) is not a God of confusion
and disorder, but of peace and order. As
(is the practice) in all the churches of the
saints (God's people)."*

This passage speaks of people prophesying, other
people judging it, other people giving a hymn or a song,
or a revelation, all at the same time. The prophetic word
is going into people's lives, opening up their lives, giving
them instruction, setting a course for their lives, exposing
things that are wrong in them. And all of this is going on
during the same service.

The Bible is saying that God, who is the source
of prophecy, is not the source of confusion and disorder,
but of peace and order.

*"If anyone thinks and claims that he
is a prophet (filled and governed by the
Holy Spirit of God, and inspired to
interpret the divine will and purpose in*

preaching or teaching) or has any other spiritual endowment, let him understand (recognize and acknowledge), that what I am writing to you is a command of the Lord."
(I Corinthians 14:37, Amplified).

Prophecy in the church is a **command of the Lord.** Let's read on:

"But if anyone disregards or does not recognize (that it is a command of the Lord), he is disregarded and not recognized (he is one whom God knows not).
So (to conclude), my brethren, earnestly desire and set your hearts on prophesying, (on being inspired to preach, and teach, and to interpret God's will and purpose), and do not forbid or hinder speaking in (unknown) tongues.
But all things should be done with regard to decency and propriety and in an orderly fashion." (I Cor. 14:38-40, Amplified).

It is clear through these scriptures that prophecy should be a regular part of church services. It shouldn't freak us out or be a weird thing. It shouldn't be a strange thing to call people out and say, "Who needs a word from the Lord?" That's proper order.

Don't let anyone discourage you from receiving prophetic words, **no one**! There is nothing wrong with wanting to know, and expecting the word of the Lord to come to you and give you direction. The Bible says in I Corinthians 14:39 to *covet, desire, go after, to lust after prophecy.*

Let me make this point with this scripture:

> **"Beware least anyone cheat you through philosophy and empty deceit, according to the tradition of men, according to the basic principles of the world, and not according to Christ."** *(Colossians 2:8)*

Beware lest anyone cheat you. No man, no woman, no preacher, no professor, no angel, no demon should be allowed to cheat or rob you of all that God has for you. Religion always tells you what you can't do and what you can't have. True Christianity empowers and encourages you with what you *can* do and what you *can* have.

Prophetic people are people who challenge. It's a **prophetic challenge** when a church begins to say, "We challenge the principalities and powers that rule over the this region."

You had better know that God told you to issue the challenge. You had also better be prepared for the "backlash" that may follow the challenge. That challenge will stir up every devil and every controlling Jezebel spirit in the territory. But the good news is that these evil spirits fear the true prophetic, because the prophetic will destroy their stronghold.

It says in I Kings 18:21,

> *"Elijah came to all the people and said, 'How long will you falter between two opinions? If the Lord is God, follow Him, but if Baal, follow him.' But the people answered him not a word."*

Now I think this is interesting because the **prophetic challenge** dealt more harshly with the principalities and powers than it did with the people. Some people need to remember this because when they begin to move in a prophetic manner, they begin to get hard, arrogant, cutting, and bitter with people. That's out of order.

The next thing we see in verse 22 is Elijah saying to the people,

> *"I alone am left a prophet of the Lord, but Baal's prophets are 450 men."*

There seems to be certain **prophetic problems** that always occur with prophetic churches. And that is, the basic feeling that "we're the ones." "We're the only ones fighting the devil." "We're the only ones really beating the principalities and powers." "We're the only ones with the anointing of God."

This may be true, but if that is your attitude, as you see in the story of Elijah, God gets tired of it and He'll take away your mantel and give it to another who doesn't have that attitude.

1. **Nowhere in the Bible does it give prophets the right to have an attitude.**
2. **Nowhere in the Bible does it give a prophet the right to be isolated.**
3. **Nowhere in the Bible does it give someone who prophesies the right to be arrogant. Nowhere!**

The Bible says, "But the fruit of the Spirit is love, joy, peace, patience, kindness, goodness, faithfulness, gentleness and self-control."

Every word that is given, every attitude that is presented, has to be tempered by the fruit of the Spirit. Otherwise, the prophet himself is out of order and is not of God, even if the word he's giving is.

"And so it was, at noon, that Elijah mocked them and said, "Cry aloud, for

he is a god; either he is meditating, or he is busy, or he is on a journey, or perhaps he is sleeping and must be awakened." I Kings 18:27

This verse is a great example of prophetic tauntings. In churches that move under the prophetic anointing, you'll notice that some of their songs may seem to **taunt** the atmosphere. Some people get freaked out about this when they go into prophetic churches. Usually the response is, "Why are they singing that song? Why are they singing against principalities and powers? Why don't they just sing about Jesus?"

Because that's part of a prophetic anointing that has strength and authority. Its gun is aimed to shoot down the works of the devil. It is done on purpose, and that's why they don't apologize for it.

We are glorifying Jesus by the testimony of Christ and the spirit of prophecy. We testify of Christ. If you don't allow **prophetic tauntings** to come on you in song, in prayer, in preaching, in prophesying, there's a measure of victory that's not going to be obtained in your own life.

Verse 30-37 speaks of Elijah rebuilding the altar. He went back and he said, "Now, before I do anything else, we're going to rebuild the altar." He set order after the false had been exposed and dealt with. He gave the glory to the "one true God!"

UNDERSTANDING THE SOURCE OF YOUR ANOINTING

There are two sources of spiritual strength, **(1)** inner strength and **(2)** outer strength. The **outer anointing** comes on you for a specific purpose. A lot of times, people rely only on the outer anointing. As long as they are witnessing and talking to other people about the Lord, they feel the Word of God stirring in them. The problem is when they're all by themselves, they don't have enough inner strength to drive off any temptation, or depression, or anything else that comes on them. That's because the inner strength, the inner anointing, the character of what you are on the inside has to be exercised. You can not rely on the anointing that you feel just when you're in a corporate prayer meeting or in a church service.

The **inner anointing**, which is what you're really made of, is what you have to learn to fight with. If you don't learn to fight the temptations and the doubts that come inside of you, you'll never be strong enough to fight outward things that are coming against you. You have to hate the tolerance of internal temptations and doubts to the same degree that you hate the devil.

We've got to learn to go inside of ourselves and deal with those things. Everybody gets excited about spiritual warfare, and our authority, and our boldness, but internally is where you begin to take your authority.

Your boldness on the inside will drive out fears, worries, doubts, insecurities, and temptations.

Your inner strength brings down the anointing of God. Your inner strength is what fights when you don't feel goosebumps. Your inner strength fights out of what's right, not because of what you feel or don't feel. It fights because a command of God is on your life to set things in order, and that's what causes you to be motivated. It is what causes you to pray when you don't feel like praying. Operating from your inner strength is really the exercising of spiritual strength.

Negative voices may respond by saying, "This is all great but the prophetic seems to stir up trouble." In spite of the negative voices, you should be able to say by personal experience, "No, the prophetic sets order."

God needs strong, loving leaders who will actually lead, instruct, warn and encourage in the prophetic. Discipleship in this way will turn negative, religious responses about the prophetic into positive, life-changing testimonies of the prophetic in operation.

The next chapter will deal with many elements of practical usage and guidelines of the personal element of prophecy.

"Anointing is simply allowing God to be in His own Word and on His own preacher. By mighty, great and continual prayerfulness, anointing is the preacher's entire potential. It inspires and clarifies his intellect, gives insight, grasps and projects power. It gives him heart power, which is greater than head power. Tenderness, purity and force flow from his heart by this anointing. Growth, freedom, fullness of thought, directness and simplicity of utterance are the result of this anointing."

E.M. Bounds, 1899

"For it is God who works in you both <u>to will</u> and <u>to do</u> for His good pleasure."
Philippians 2:13

PART IV

Let's Get Practical

Chapter 10

Activation for the Local Church

Being educated about the prophetic, and stirred to operate in it, is just a part of what is needed. Now let's look at some practical applications to incorporating the prophetic into your local church and your personal life. This chapter will reveal some easy-to-follow guidelines according to scripture for releasing and judging prophecies.

8 STEPS TO RELEASING THE PROPHETIC

1. **You must develop a close, personal relationship with the Lord.** The Holy Spirit is the source from

which you draw. If you do not know Him, you will not be able to speak for Him. (James 4:7-8)

2. **Walk in the love of God and always strive to operate with a right heart towards His people.** The love of God is the propeller behind the boat. Anything less will allow mixtures of the flesh and the devil to be released as prophecies are given. It was the love of God that gave us His Son and all the benefits that came with our salvation. It must be love that we operate in according to His Spirit. God is love! (I Corinthians 13:1-8)

3. **Sincerely and earnestly desire to prophecy!** We must desire the good gifts of God that are promised and freely given to us all. (I Corinthians 14:1)

4. **Always be sensitive to the Spirit and obediently respond to His prompting.** Remember, there is grace for you if you miss the timing of the Lord or don't respond at all. However, learn from it and be quick to respond the next time. Build a trust between you and the Holy Spirit. When He speaks, you must trust Him and be bold to step out and give the prophetic utterance. The more often you are faithful and obedient, the more He will use you as a trusted vessel of honor. (I John 2:20,23,27)

5. **Resist the fear of man and activate your faith to prophesy.** *"The fear of man brings a snare, but those who trust in the Lord will be secure."* (Proverbs 29:25) To fear man over God is a sin. We can not serve two masters, God and man. Our love and compassion for people combined with our desire to serve and love God will help us to step out in faith and prophesy.

6. **Keep yourself filled with and stirred up in the Holy Spirit.** This will only come through a consistent, personal prayer life that is not stale, but is rich with the presence of God, and by staying filled with the Word of God. You must also be committed to a local church in order to know what God is doing in that house. As you step out in prophecy, it should agree with and confirm the vision and the message that God has given to the leadership of that church, and you have to be present to do that. If you don't attend church, how can anyone trust you or know the fruit of your life-style which are the very things that will qualify you to speak and be received? (Ephesians 5:15-21)

7. **Be bold, step out, and speak the word of the Lord that has been "quickened" in you by the Holy Spirit at the appropriate time of the service.** You will develop boldness as you spend time with God and are filled with the fear of the Lord. Some

of the manifestations of being baptized in the Holy Spirit are boldness, love for the brethren, and having Him tell you things that you did not know. All of these manifestations are needful when operating in the prophetic. (Acts 4:13)

8. **Regularly practice and exercise the gift of prophecy, and it will develop you in the realm of the prophetic.** The more you do it, the easier it is and the more accurate you become. Like any kind of exercise, you will develop your spiritual muscles by regularly doing it.

HELPFUL HINTS ABOUT PROPHECY

1. **The operation of all gifts of the Spirit, including prophecy, are subject to pastoral oversight.** God has placed the pastor over the local flock to watch for and guard against human error, the threat of a wolf, and to make sure that proper development and growth occur individually and corporately. Every believer should be willing and submitted to the idea of having his or her prophecies tested according to the Word of God.

2. **The utterance gifts (the vocal ones) should be administered at the right time and in the right tone or spirit.** God is not the author of confusion,

disorder, or rude interruptions. The Holy Spirit will not supersede a person's will and "make them" do or say anything. Therefore, the excuse of "God just made me do it," is not an appropriate answer for disruption. There will be a "flow" of the anointing. This means that it will be a smooth and agreeable transition. (I Corinthians 14:33)

3. **Never lecture or beat up the sheep all in the name of prophecy.** Prophecy is for edifying, exhorting, and comforting. (I Corinthians 14:3) That doesn't mean that every prophecy will be "warm and fuzzy." A person can be comforted, exhorted and edified by a strong word of prophecy that may confirm, empower or impart something into their life. Don't limit God, just have pure motives. Be free from emotional or soulish mixtures in your delivery and have a true love for the people.

4. **Steer away from screaming, shouting, or strange physical movements while attempting to prophesy.** These type of actions draw more attention to you than to the message that God wants to deliver to His people. On the other hand, make sure you do not speak so softly that no one can hear you. Be confident, but stay humble and never draw your identity from the gift or from being used in prophecy. **A godly character will always supercede a title.**

5. <u>**Know when to quit.**</u> It is a harmful thing to become wrapped up in emotions when prophesying. This will cause you to go past the will or exact word from God. Speak only what is of the Spirit and not your flesh. Jesus said He spoke only what he heard the Father speak. (John 8:28)

6. <u>**Never use "pet" doctrines, personal opinions, recent arguments, or preferred Bible revelations as a source of prophecy.**</u> Prophecy is not your platform to preach or make a point. Remain faithful to give out what the Spirit of God is quickening you to give. Bear trustworthy fruit and never take advantage of or misuse this free gift. (John 8:28,47)

7. <u>**Avoid lots of repetition in your message or phrases.**</u> If the contents of your prophecies are always the same, then you have missed God. Carefully discern the difference between what God is saying to you personally and what He would use you to say to the congregation. Also, concerning repetition, don't get into a habit of saying things like, *"My children," "And the Lord would say," "Thus saith the Lord," "Yea, My little lambs,"* etc.

<u>**MOST IMPORTANTLY**</u>
<u>***"DO NOT DESPISE PROPHESYING!"***</u>
(I Thessalonians 5:20)

GUIDELINES FOR PROPERLY JUDGING PROPHECY

We see from scripture that all believers should be submitted to the spiritual authority of the church in having his or her prophecies judged. This is not to say that we are to operate from a critical or controlling spirit, but rather understand that Paul exhorted the elders of the church to guard and protect the flock of God (I Thessalonians 5:19-21 and I Corinthians 14:29). There should be grace and teaching available when mistakes are made, because mistakes will be made along the way. But a heart for accuracy that is submitted to godly leadership will bear much fruit and be honored by God.

Take a look at these seven questions to ask when judging prophecy:

1. **Does it agree with the Word of God?** The Bible is the final authority and the standard for our lives and the methods of our churches. (Proverbs 30:5-6; Titus 1:9:2 Timothy 3:16)

2. **Does it exalt and bring glory to Jesus?** Prophecies that exalt man, organizations or doctrines do not lift up Jesus. The Holy Spirit will always bring glory and honor to Jesus. (John 16:13-14, Revelation 19:10)

3. **Does it bear witness with your spirit and/or the spirit of those in the congregation?** One of the manifestations of being filled with the Spirit is the confirmation or inner witness He plants on the inside of us. *"In a multitude of counselors there is safety."* (Proverbs 24:6) If you are unsure about a prophecy, it is best to just "put it on a shelf," pray about it, and see if it comes to pass.

4. **Does it edify, encourage and/or comfort?** If you are left with confusion, condemnation, doubt, fear, anger, or frustration, then the prophecy was not from God. God is not the author of any of these things. (I Corinthians. 14:3, 2 Timothy 3:16; I Corinthians 14:33)

5. **Does it produce freedom and liberty, or bondage and containment?** God is the giver of life! *Where the Spirit of the Lord is there is liberty! God's grace is sufficient* for all of us. *God has not given us a spirit of fear, but of power, love and a sound mind.* The Bible is full of freedom filled answers to this question. (Romans 8:15; II Corinthians 3:17)

6. **Does the fruit or life of the one giving the prophecy reflect the character of Christ?** If the life of the person giving out the prophecy is full of sin, out of order, rebellious, and the like,

then that person should not be allowed to prophesy over the congregation until such a time as reconciliation and progress has been made in that person's heart and life. (Galatians 5:22,23; Matthew 7:16-18) The Bible likewise tells us to *"know those who labor among you."* (1 Thessalonians 5:12) This is an important fact to consider when receiving prophecy personally or allowing prophecy to be given over the congregation.

7.   **Does the prophecy come to pass?**   Prophecy is a foretelling of something to come and/or the confirmation of the will of God. Prophecy also reveals the hearts of men. If the word spoken never comes to pass, is not fulfilled, or is untrue, then how can we attribute it to God? *For God is not a man that He should lie.* If we ask Him for bread, He doesn't give us a stone.

Remember the Bible tells us not to be ignorant of spiritual gifts. Don't avoid prophecy or any other gift just because of a lack of knowledge or a previous bad experience. Allow the Lord to teach you and your church in this area. Allow room for grace and room for mistakes as you are learning and practicing. *"Earnestly desire spiritual gifts but especially that you may prophesy." (1 Corinthians 14:1)*

Chapter 11

Daily Applications of the Gift

The gifts of the Spirit can and should operate in your life on a daily basis. They should be active on the job, at home, in the grocery store, in the restaurant, as well as in the church. (Acts 17:16-17 & Acts 5:42) The following are key things to the accurate, proper and effective use of the gifts of the Spirit.

1. **Attitude:** Our attitude in using the gifts of the Spirit must be one prompted by the love of God in order to bless people. This is the reason we operate in the gifts, to give to others by the unction of the Holy

Ghost. We cannot be mixed with selfish motives and purposes and expect God to allow us to speak on His behalf.

2. **Sensitivity:** You must be aware of the people around you, the atmosphere, and the prompting of the Holy Spirit while you are ministering. We must maintain our position as a "watchman on the wall" at all times. Opportunities to be used of God are always available. God is always speaking, are you listening? **Awareness of what is going on around us will assist in the proper timing and activation of the gifts, and which gift is the best to use for that particular situation.** You must become spiritually fit and prepared to be used when the opportunity arises to do so. It may take practice to develop the capacity to be sensitive to the Holy Spirit.

3. **Application:** Know which gift to use and how to use it. We do not have to make an announcement or identify the type of gift or prompting we are receiving to be effective. Oftentimes, when dealing with unbelievers, it is helpful to speak out what the Lord has given to you in an understandable way, void of religious phrasing and jargon.

4. **Focus:** Stay aware of what is going on while being used of the Lord. This simply means to notice the response of those you are ministering to. If laying

hands on someone, it is a good idea not to close your eyes while praying for them so that you can stay attuned to their reaction as well as your surroundings.

5. **Following Through:** As you are watching for the person's spiritual and natural reaction, listen to the Holy Spirit and be prepared to follow through with further instructions. Know when to take advantage of an opportunity to continue ministering or speaking into the person's life.

6. **Affirmation:** Always give encouragement when needed. This is extremely important when ministering to people that you have a continued relationship with such as co-workers, family members, church members, etc.

The gifts of the Holy Spirit are many and varied. They can be applied in a multitude of ways, independently and in conjunction with each other. The scriptural mandate is to not be ignorant of spiritual gifts and to use them. Just like the parable of the talent, to use spiritual gifts is to experience an increase in the areas of accuracy, boldness, spiritual capacity and maturity; however, to deny the activation of spiritual gifts would result in the decrease or stagnation of those areas in your spiritual growth.

The Holy Spirit is calling for Christians to be Christians beyond the four walls of the church. It's time to take dominion, and we have been equipped with His supernatural power and the gifts of the Spirit for that purpose.

Chapter 12

The Snares of a Young Prophet

A prophetic gift plus zeal, plus boldness, plus inexperience, plus immaturity, plus underdevelopment, equals a possible disaster to the likes of an up-and-coming prophet of God. Common mistakes can be avoided with a little wisdom, and by taking one step at a time. Let's take a look at some familiar pits that a young prophet could quite easily fall into if gone unnoticed:

1. **Presumption:** Most prophets are high speed, highly motivated individuals, and are not always "tempered" in their prophetic gift. A common mistake is that they hear something from God and presume it is a

"now" word, or that today, or better yet, yesterday, would have been the perfect time for the word to be made manifest. What this prophet or prophetess needs is a good, strong, loving pastor to be used by God to bring maturity, development and tempering to their gift so they don't burn themselves out and everyone around them.

Pastors and prophets should be able to function together with great compatibility. Most young prophets think that the word "temper" means compromise or becoming watered-down. This is not true. **The word "temper" simply means to deliver the message with the right heart and a right attitude.** <u>Temperance and accuracy go hand in hand.</u> Prophets should be able to compliment the gift of the pastor and submit to the authority of the pastor.

2. <u>**Fear of Man:**</u> The Bible says that the *"fear of man brings a <u>snare</u>"* (Proverbs 29:25). There is a fine line between giving a prophetic word seasoned with grace and the character of God, and battling against the temptation of fearing or being a man-pleaser. **Some prophetic words are not exactly pleasing to hear, but if the timing is right, hearts are right, and the love of God is present, the results will bring freedom.** Caring too much about every little thing someone thinks or says can handicap a prophet. That is why accuracy must be adhered to. Some

young prophets are too hard, and some are too timid. The point is to find the balance not through your mind, emotions, or past experiences, but by the Spirit of God.

3. **Inferiority:** Whenever you see or hear someone cut down others to build themselves up, there is an inferiority complex present. This produces a critical spirit and a habitual behavior pattern. The answer is found in humility, which is found through repentance. The root to all of this is pride, which I have addressed specifically just a few paragraphs away. **A prophet must be delivered from inferiority in order to be effective and not harmful.** Don't allow insecurity to cause you to be hypersensitive to criticism. Ask the Holy Spirit to discern the criticism, make any changes necessary, or just disregard it. Persecution will come, but sometimes God will use it to produce stability and a greater confidence in Him.

4. **Rejection:** Rejection is very common in the lives of many prophets. Oftentimes they have been rejected by not only those they attempted to minister to in the past, but by other ministry gifts, friends and family members who felt threatened or did not understand the prophetic. Because prophets are highly driven, zealous people, they also carry themselves in a naturally authoritative way. These qualities can be quite intimidating at times. As a result, people have a

tendency to reject them for fear of being pulled out of their own comfort zones. **It is imperative that a prophet not carry this rejection around on the inside of them. It is detrimental to the gift and call of God on their life.** Rejection will cripple not only the prophet, but all those they leave in their wake. This is why it is so important to have temperance, a right heart, and to be secure in who you are in Christ. These victorious qualities will allow you to discern the dysfunctions of others without being affected by them, then you can minister to them accordingly.

5. **<u>Spiritual Pride:</u>** Excessive boasting in the revelations that God has given you, or the way in which He used you to minister, is like a neon sign that reads, "Pride lives here." Testimonies are great and powerful, but when every sentence that comes from your mouth starts with "I," then there is problem. **If you can't sit still and listen to the testimonies of others without boasting about yourself, then you are guilty of the sin of spiritual pride.**

When you receive a prophetic revelation or give a prophetic word out, don't glory in "your" revelation or "your" word. If what you receive comes from heaven, you don't own it or hold the exclusive rights to it. We are to edify, encourage, build up, and impart to the Body of Christ. We don't become an individual entity.

Allow the revelations and words that you give out to become alive (*rhema*) in the lives of others. **Prophets shouldn't profit from the bondage of others, but instead should produce freedom by ministering a timely word from God to His people.**

6. <u>Independent:</u> Many prophets find it challenging and sometimes impossible to be a part of a local church. We all have a war story about being misunderstood and unaccepted. However, some prophets refuse to submit to a pastor because of past rejection or pride. This is a big mistake and a very haughty, self-righteous attitude to have. **The prophet should repent for this attitude and pray that God will send him or her to the right church with divine, accurate leadership.** Maybe the pastor isn't as progressive in the realm of the prophetic as you are, but he will care deeply for the flock (including you) and have great wisdom that you need to draw from.

There is an age-old conflict between prophets and pastors. Prophets are often very critical and judgmental of pastors, causing pastors to pull away. Thus, the walls are formed and rejection continues to live on. No five-fold minister or gift of the spirit was ever destined to be a "Lone Ranger." It doesn't work that way. **Five-fold ministries and gifts of the spirit are for the *equipping of the saints for*** *the work of the ministry,* **that the body can** *be* *fitly joined together, each member doing its part.*

Isolation only opens the door to the devil. Be open to the counsel of pastors. Be patient with one another and don't make hasty decisions because of a rocky relationship or past hurts. **Make sure it is God's voice of direction you are following and not the voice of the enemy drawing you away to make you easy prey.**

Chapter 13

Things to Remember

When prophesying or ministering prophetically we must remember there are several factors to consider in order to effectively line up with God's perfect will and express His heart:

In God's kingdom, similar to the secular world, our level of authority has everything to do with our **level of responsibility.** Our level of authority or circle of influence will only be as great or as far-reaching as our willingness to accept responsibility. **Authority, or qualification, does not come from "revelation," it comes from responsibility and faithfulness.** Sometimes God will allow us to see in the spirit beyond our position or ability to deal with a particular situation, but that does not give us a license to step out and assume a position we do not have. When this is the case, deliver your revelation or insight to leadership, allow them to use their discretion in the execution of that revelation, and most of all trust God with the outcome. If we do not act according to this manner, division will come instead of unity.

Humility is a huge factor in delivering any word of prophecy to anyone, especially leadership. **Our level of authority effects how we express our revelations and with whom we are to share those revelations.** It is helpful to communicate how or at what level we received the prophetic word or revelation, whether by:
- dream
- vision
- impression
- audible word
- written word
- internal knowing, etc.

This will assist in bringing a greater clarification in the delivery and the reception of the word, since those being ministered to are responsible to judge the word. Don't always just claim that "God spoke to me." These types of generalizations could bring confusion, again causing division.

Make sure that you communicate how much or little you understand of what you have received from the Spirit, so as not to mislead or go into a detailed interpretation other than what you have **understanding** of. **Remember to only give what you have actually received.** Our purpose is not to cause confusion, but to encourage and strengthen.

The Bible instructs us to *prophesy according to the proportion of our faith.* (Romans 12:6) Not only should we prophesy in **proportion to our faith** and be content with where we are in that, but also we should **prophesy in faith.** Incorporate prayers of faith and confession into your prophecy, especially when you have been shown something like a sickness or a cycle of weakness or bondage in someone's life.

Most importantly, **be motivated by love!** Prophecy is in fact a message from God, but don't ever forget that it is towards His children. Prophets and prophecy are not to come across angry, harsh, or destructive. Although the word may be strong, it must be administered in love. *"The testimony of Jesus is the spirit of prophecy."* (Revelation 19:10) Jesus is the perfect picture of sacrificial love to mankind. Our prophetic ministry must contain hope. God is not the god of hopelessness. He gives us hope that takes away our shame.

ROOM FOR MISTAKES

Fear of failure seems to be the number one reason that believers resist the desire to prophesy, miss God, or never recover after one or more mistakes. God's grace and accurate leadership will always leave room for growth, which means you may make some mistakes along the way. Remember these things as you develop this area of your spiritual life:

1. The voice of God is never the voice that says, "You're a failure." The Holy Ghost brings conviction; the devil brings condemnation. Recognize the difference and give credit where credit is due.

2. You must be willing to step out in the company of others, even at the risk of failure, and trust in God.

3. Never allow mistakes to handicap you. Get back up on the horse and continue to ride! *"A righteous man falls seven times and rises again."* (Proverbs 24:16)

4. Start where you are and allow the Lord to develop you further, making the applicable changes along the way. You must be teachable.

5. Be quick to admit your mistake, repent, learn from it, and go on! That is the formula for spiritual progression.

Speaking forth a word or prophecy is just the first step. You also must allow the Lord to teach you and season you to **interpret** and **apply** words and prophecies. The above five principles apply to these

<u>two functions as well.</u> The utterance, the interpretation and the application are all encompassing within the Body of Christ. Maybe God didn't use you to "give" the prophecy, but He might use you to interpret it. **Whether giving or interpreting a prophecy, all are responsible to apply the accurate word of the Lord.**

In conclusion, we need to begin finding out the way the Spirit of the Lord wants to use us. How do you find that out? You have to exercise yourself by stepping out and doing new things.

Look for opportunities to exercise spiritual gifts. There are plenty of opportunities. Imagine that you decide you want to compete in the Mr. America contest. If that's something that you really desire, it's going to take some work. That means there's going to be a lot of days in the gym. There are going to be a lot of days you don't feel like working out. If you're going to continue to get to the place of obtaining what you are pursuing, then on the days you don't feel like "exercising," you have to do it anyway. You're also going to have those days when you feel weak, but you press forward and do what you need to do, because you're pursuing that particular goal. *If you fail, have a bad day, or miss the mark, don't stop! Get up and keep going. Press toward the mark of the high calling in Christ Jesus.*

IF YOU WANT MORE

If you want to begin flowing more in the gift of prophecy, pray this simple prayer from your heart:

"Heavenly Father, I thank you for Your Word. Father, I've read in Your Word that I should desire spiritual gifts, and especially to prophesy. So Lord, I won't be rebellious, and I won't be lazy, but I desire Your spiritual gifts. I desire to prophesy because You said all shall prophesy. Jesus, You paid a big price to release these gifts into the earth, and I too want them to flow through me. Help me, by the Spirit of God, to begin to exercise myself in the spiritual gym of the Holy Ghost, to prophesy and to move out in the gifts of the Spirit. From this day, by faith, I shall flow in prophecy, in the prophetic realms, in realms of revelation, in realms of knowledge, in realms of spiritual gifts. You told me to covet these things. So Lord, I stir myself up, as a believer in Jesus Christ, to have all the things that You provided for me as weapons, as tools, and as equipment for survival in this earth, and in my Christian life. In Jesus Name, I thank You."

"If you take away the New Testament pattern of the church, it's subject to man's opinions, doctrines and creeds. Then God must send apostolic reformers to re-establish the pattern."

Barry A. Cook

"... Your sons and your daughters shall prophesy."
Joel 2:28

"...having been built on the foundation of the apostles and prophets..."
Ephesians 2:19-22

"...For the testimony of Jesus is the spirit of prophecy."
Revelation 19:7-10

"...desire earnestly to prophesy."
I Corinthians 14:39

"Do not despise prophecies... Test all things..."
I Thessalonians 5:20-21

"...to root out, to pull down: To destroy, to throw down to build and to plant..."
Jeremiah 1:10

"...to another prophecy..."
I Corinthians 12:7-10

"...especially that you may prophesy...prophecies speak edification, exhortation and comfort to men."
I Corinthians 14:1-3

"Do not neglect the gift that is in you which was given to you by prophecy..."
I Timothy 4:14-16

"I wish you all spoke with tongues but even more that you prophesy."
I Corinthians 14:5

"...no prophecy of scripture is of any private interpretation..."
II Peter 1:19-21

"...wage war according to the prophecies given unto you..."
I Timothy 1:18

"...and let the others judge (while the rest pay attention and weigh and discern what is said)... For you can all prophesy (for in this way you can give testimony)... desire earnestly and set your hearts on prophesying (on being inspired to preach and teach and to interpret God's will and purpose)..."
I Corinthians 14:29-40 (AMP)

"... let us prophesy in proportion to our faith..."
Romans 12:6

"If ALL prophesy..."
I Corinthians 14:24

To contact the author
Write to:
Barry A. Cook
Battlecry Outreach Ministries
4055 Oceanside Blvd. Suite T
Oceanside, CA 92056

To receive other materials by Barry Cook, please send your pre-paid order to the above address or call (760) 639-4000 for more information.
(Free Shipping & Handling)

With each order you will receive a free copy of "Apprehended by God." This booklet is an excellent source of ministry for the unsaved and backslidden heart!

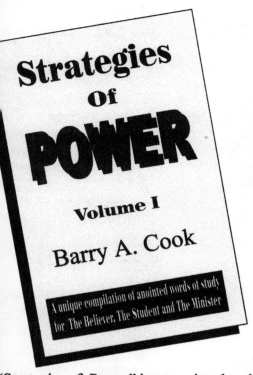

"Strategies of Power" is an anointed tool of study to assist the believer, the student and the minister with outlines of reforming messages for today's generation. I believe the information in Volume One of this book will impart valuable keys to empower you to press towards the high call of God for your life and ministry.

In Volume One of "Strategies of Power" you will be equipped by life changing messages, such as:

8 Attributes Of A True Apostle
10 Biblical Characteristics Of A Prophetic Church
How To Deliver A Spirit Filled Sermon
Know the Difference Between A Secular Church And A Spiritual
Church
Excellence In Ministry Checklist
10 Reasons Why All Believers Should Speak In Other Tongues
There are 3 Types of People In Every Church, Which One Are You?
7 Steps To Bring Change To Any Circumstance
35 Ways To Help Activate The Miraculous...and many more.

Make this valuable resource a part of your library today!

SINGLES

$5 Each

Spirit Life

____Revelation Knowledge
____Repentance - The Key To Revival
____Key That Bring His Presence
____Spiritual Momentum
____Being Sensitive to the Holy Spirit
____The Emotions of the Holy Spirit
____Pastoring in the Spirit
____Lifestyle of Evangelism
____The Devil's Worst Nightmare
____The Devil's Worst Nightmare Part 2
____Response Determines Release
____Daily in the Temple
____The Wind Blows Where it May
____Fruits of Repentance
____Overcoming the Voice of Discouragement
____Recover your Anointing
____Apprehended By God
____Stirred to Action
____Authority to Stand
____Spirit Led People
____Conquering Compromise in His presence
____Keep Your Sense of Urgency
____Living the Anointed Life
____Obtaining God's Promises in the Wilderness
____Faith That Possesses

Apostolic & Prophetic

____Cry of Reformation
____Process of Restoration
____Process of Establishing Truth
____The Prophetic Church
____Apostolic Anointing
____Apostolic Christianity
____Prophetic Functions
____Taking the Land
____Divine Strategy for Taking the Area
____Building the Character of Reform
____Stand Your Ground
____No More Compromise

Issues of Today

____President Clinton's Gospel
____Rising To A New Level
____Stand Still, Hold On & Hush Up
____How To Walk Away From Lack
____What is Backlash?
____#1 Reason Why Relationships F
____Foundation of a Strong Church
____Battle at the Gates
____The Law of First Things
____Spirit of the Area: Pride
____Christ the Anointed One
____Occupy till He Comes
____Carrying the Spirit of Revival
____Profiting in the Midst
____Divine Order
____The Fear of God
____Destroying the Traditions of
the Elders: Part 1
____Destroying the Traditions of
the Elders: Part 2
____No More Excuses
____The Charge of the Lord
____Doers of the Word
____Prejudice & Racism
____No Prejudice Allowed
____Love or Duty
____10 Fundamentals of Christian Li
____Marks of a Backslidden Heart
____Anointing on Governments
____Becoming a Champion
____Sacrifice of the Heart
____The Heart of a Warrior

NEW RELEASES

AUDIO ALBUMS

____Vision $10.00
Tapes Include: Vision Destroyers
                Press On - Hold to the Vision

____We Need A Deliverer $15.00
Tapes Include: We Need A Deliverer
               You Must Make a Stand
               Functions of a Deliverer

____4th Quarter Christian $15.00
Tapes Include: 4th Quarter Christian
                Exposing Cultural Strongholds
                Characteristics of 4th Quarter Christian

____Breaking Ungodly Soul Ties $15.00
Tapes Include: Be Loosed
                Breaking Ungodly Soul Ties
                Characteristic of Soul Ties

____Grace - *Does it press your forward or push you back?* $20.00
Tapes Include: The Grace Factor
                Amazing Grace
                The Working of Grace
                A Different Look at the Prodigal

____Crisis - *A Force for Increase!* $20.00
Tapes Include: The Benefits to Crisis
               How to Get through a Crisis
               Staying Focused During a Storm
               Why People Forsake

"Single tapes from audio albums may be purchased separately for $5.00 each."

AUDIO ALBUMS

___Faith That Obtains Promises (2 Tapes) $10.00

___Going Through the Fire Without Getting Burnt
(2 Tapes) $ 10.00

___Pathway to Breakthrough (2 Tapes) $10.00

___Living in The Realm of The Spirit $15.00
Tapes Include: Depth Training
Living in the Glory,
The Depths of God

___Divine Press $20.00
Tapes Include: Divine Press
Keeping the Press 1 & 2
Setting up the Standard

___Radical Christianity $20.00
Tapes Include: God is Working in the Background
Kicking in the Gates of Hell
Holy Ghost Worship
Let's Get Radical

___Spiritual Momentum $20.00
Tapes Include: Church Lite
Crossing to Victory
Accelerating Your Destiny
Turn Your Anger Into Action

___The Ministry of Helps $20.00
Tapes Include: The Spiritual Function of Helps
The Role of Music in Helps
Intercession and Faith
Working in the Spirit of The Leader

___The New Breed Church $20.00
Tapes Include: Church Lite
Untouchables: Making a Distinct Sound
Secular Church vs Spiritual Church
Apostolic Reformers Today
Containers of the Presence of God
CHURCH - Not What it Used to Be

___The Spirit of The Area: Divination $20.00
Tapes Include: Spirit of The Area Divination,
Exposing Strongholds
Religion: Round One
Keeping An Open Heavens

____**Study of the New Testament Church,
Mad, Sad or Glad $20.00**
Tapes Include: Mad, Sad Glad,
                Victory Over Control
                Apostolic Church
                The Church, Unstoppable & Immovable

____**Origin Of The Apostle $20.00**
Tapes Include: The Historical Dimension Of The Apostle
                Understanding, Boundaries, Administrations
                  and Offices
                The Functions Of The Apostle
                Apostolic Warfare Ministry

____**23 Principles of the Apostolic Mandate $20.00**
Tapes Include: Principles of an Apostolic Mandate
                Parts I, II, and III

____**The Power of Prayer $20.00**
Tapes Include: The High Call of Prayer
                Why Pray in Tongues
                Strong Prayer
                Persistent Prayer

____**Strategies For Strong Christian Living $30.00**
Tapes Include: The Spirit Of The Father
                True Fatherly Anointing
                Darlings or Demons?
                Brats or Blessings?
                Take This Job and Love It Parts 1 & 2

____**Never Struggle With Your Mind Again $30.00**
Tapes Include: Renewing Your Mind & Strengthening Your Will
                Characteristics of a Sound Mind
                The Spirit of Your Mind
                Renewing Your Mind; Factor of the Flesh
                15 Benefits of a Renewed Mind

Live Praise & Worship
____**Fresh Fire   Cassette $8.00 / CD $12.00**

Books
____*Apprehended By God (pocket book)*	*$ 2.00*
____*Strategies of Power - Volume I*	*$ 5.00*

AUDIO ALBUMS

Notes

<u>Notes</u>

<u>Notes</u>